Teaching Shakespeare—
Yes You Can!

by Lorraine Hopping Egan

S C H O L A S T I C
PROFESSIONAL **B**OOKS

NEW YORK • TORONTO • LONDON • AUCKLAND • SYDNEY

Acknowledgments

The author would like to thank Molly Haws
for steering me off the primrose path of ignorance
and giving me rhyme or reason
whenever I was without.

Cover design by Jaime Lucero and Vincent Ceci
Cover illustration by Mona Mark
Interior design by Solutions by Design, Inc.
Interior illustrations by Mona Mark
Poster illustrations by Michael Moran

ISBN 0-590-37401-X

Copyright © 1998 by Lorraine Hopping Egan

Printed in the U.S.A

Contents

ACT III: *The Plot Thickens*

Exploring the play post-reading or performing

Reproducibles:

ACT IV: *Meet the Elizabethans*

Shakespeare and his world

Reproducibles:

ACT V: *Infinite Jest*

Resources for further enjoyment of Shakespeare

POSTER: *Will-Spoken*

Is It Possible to Teach Shakespeare to Middle School Students? Yes!

When I gave a middle school teacher a book called *Shakespeare Insults for Teachers* (see Resources, page 77), she plunged in wholeheartedly—and then stopped cold.

"Why doesn't he just speak English?" my friend half joked. Then, in the next breath, "My sixth graders would *love* this."

The lure of motivating students to read by using clever put-downs overpowered her initial resistance to unfamiliar words. My friend mined some choice nuggets for her class to decipher and rewrite into compliments (see Rude Dude on page 14).

This encounter illustrates the fundamental question of this book: If well-educated adults are intimidated by the language, is it possible to teach Shakespeare to middle school students? Answer: When properly motivated, even by insults, children (and adults) will tackle almost any text. Readability formulas are tossed out the window. Short attention spans suddenly become longer. Hard words don't seem so hard.

This book offers creative, highly motivating activities that work for almost any Shakespeare play. I have provided examples and models from a variety of plays, including the often overlooked comedies, along with ideas for independent or small-group projects across the curriculum. Many of the activities also include a ready-to-use reproducible.

Whereas the activities provide specific tips for making Shakespeare a success in your classroom, here are several general tips.

Show What They Know

Children already know Shakespeare; they just might not know that they know it:

- Check out the famous phrases on the "Will-Spoken" poster.

- Each day, recite a famous line—"To be or not to be . . ."; "Alas, poor Yorick"; "A horse! A horse! My kingdom for a horse!" Use the "Will-Spoken" poster as a source.

- Play Tchaikovsky's *Romeo and Juliet* overture and see how many milliseconds it takes for students to recognize the melody.

- Ask students to draw a picture—any picture—that means "Shakespeare" to them; compare this "before" picture with an "after" picture drawn at the end of the unit.

- Discuss, screen, or watch stage performances of contemporary versions of the plays, such as *West Side Story* (*Romeo and Juliet*), *Just One of the Guys* (*Twelfth Night*), and *Ran* (*King Lear*).

- ❧ If all else fails, tell students to watch *Batman* reruns on Nick at Nite. Alfred the butler opens the bat cave by moving a bust of—guess who?—William Shakespeare!

Broaden the Repertoire

Most schools teach *Hamlet, Romeo and Juliet, Macbeth,* or *Julius Caesar*, all four of which are tragedies. What, no comedies?

Shakespeare's comedies are generally shorter, easier to read, and more fun for children to perform. The themes also tend to be less "adult" and the plots less violent.

For example, *Twelfth Night* is about a long-lost twin brother and sister who find each other after much mayhem and mistaken identity. In *A Midsummer Night's Dream*, two young couples run away to a wacky fairy world. The plot of *Much Ado About Nothing* revolves around two practical jokes that students may have experienced firsthand. *As You Like It* features a gender-switching heroine and a wild party in a forest.

Have Serious Fun and Games

Turning lessons into games can take the edge off of almost any difficult subject. Several games in this book teach or review character, plot, theme, and language. A commercial board game called The Play's the Thing (see page 77) does the same.

Don't Believe You Have to Do the Whole Thing

With Shakespeare, quality and depth are better than quantity and breadth. Rather than tackle the entire text of a play, summarize parts as needed and concentrate on a meaty act or scene.

You can choose scenes that are sure to hook kids and pass over scenes that aren't essential to the main plot. You'll have time to reread, recite, and decipher passages in greater depth. Most important, students will feel less intimidated by the reduced amount of text and will gain a sense of confidence as they more easily master it.

Give 'Em a Break

Children can enjoy and learn from a play without understanding every word. Elizabethan audiences probably didn't either, especially since Shakespeare invented many words. Even Shakespeare scholars can't interpret the entire text.

So rather than belabor difficult parts, emphasize the whole. Allow students to feel good about reading Shakespeare in the first place. They'll willingly fill in the blanks later on.

Stand Up and Act Out

Shakespeare's plays were not even published until after his death. The only way to know them was to see and hear them onstage.

For this reason, more Shakespeare programs are emphasizing dramatic presentation over literary scholarship. This doesn't mean that you have to stage a complete production of *Hamlet* with your class. Instead, read the play aloud in class and ask students to take different parts. Encourage them to really ham it up and let everyone know what a character is feeling and saying. Keep in mind that students have experienced rhythmic language from Dr. Seuss to modern rap. They love talking to a beat.

Put Pageantry in the Limelight

The costumes, staging, and traditions of Elizabethan drama are not just bit parts of a Shakespeare unit. As major players, these theatrical trappings can stir children's imaginations and sow fond, lifelong memories about studying Shakespeare. To wit:

Dress up for a masked ball! Fake a dying scene, complete with stage blood and famous last words! Play Elizabethan music while you work! Dance an Elizabethan jig! Invite professional stage fighters or fencers to perform.

NOTATION GUIDE

Plays are cited using the following notation.

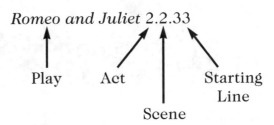

Turn to act 2, scene 2, line 33 of *Romeo and Juliet* to read a famous line. Note that line numbers vary slightly from edition to edition.

The Play's the Thing

Wherein the players (your students) prepare for reading and performing the text with exercises, activities, and projects.

Who's Got the Rhythm?

An introduction to blank verse.

PURPOSE

Students read and examine a short passage to discover the rhythm of blank verse.

BACKGROUND INFORMATION

Shakespeare wrote his plays in prose, blank verse (unrhymed iambic pentameter), and rhymed verse. He used these different poetic forms to help convey and clarify ideas to his audience. For example, the poetic form emphasizes a character's rank, reveals a state of mind, or reflects a turn of events.

In Shakespeare's plays, working-class characters generally speak in prose—unless they're imitating nobles. Noble characters usually speak in blank verse—unless they go mad or lose their rank; then they may switch to prose. (Note that in some plays, particularly his later ones, Shakespeare made greater use of prose.)

The rhythm of blank verse is iambic pentameter. *Iamb* is Greek for a two-syllable foot (section) of a line; pentameter means "a measure of five." Thus, *iambic pentameter* has five iambs (10 syllables) per line.

The syllables normally have a simple cadence: da DA da DA da DA da DA da DA. If this rhythm is slightly skewed, it is often a reflection of the character's state of mind. One example is Mercutio's manic "Queen Mab" speech in *Romeo and Juliet* (1.4.54). For another, compare Richard II's perfect iambic pentameter speech to Northumberland (3.2.72) to his shaky speech after being deposed, imprisoned, and driven mad (5.5.1).

Watch out for words with a changed stress (blessED instead of BLESSed), an added syllable (a-swearing instead of swearing), or a dropped syllable (do't instead of do it). Elizabethan pronunciation differed enough that some lines will sound offbeat when spoken with an American accent.

The highest form of poetry, rhymed verse, is reserved for the most noble characters, spirits such as fairies, and songs. A rhymed couplet signals the end of a scene. Supernaturals such as Puck sometimes speak in eight-syllable lines: IF we SHAdows HAVE offENDed.

These definitions are here for you to use at your discretion. Students don't necessarily need to know this terminology to read Shakespeare, but they do need to recognize the different rhythms.

WHAT TO DO

Start this activity by making a copy of the Who's Got the Rhythm? reproducible on page 20. Using the hash marks as a guide, cut out each small section of text and distribute one section per student. Depending on the number of students in your class, you can adjust the length of the speech to fit your class size. Other suitable passages from *Romeo and Juliet* include the prologue and the prince's first speech (1.1.81). (You can also choose an iambic pentameter passage from a play you are or will be reading in class.)

Ask students to read their section of text and raise their hands if they don't understand a word. Going randomly around the room, ask each student to stand and read his or her phrase aloud.

Correct any obvious or gross mispronunciations, but leave the fine-tuning for later.

Next, collect the phrases and write the first line of the passage across the board. Write each syllable separately, making the stressed syllables all caps. Ask for ten volunteers to stand in front of the board, each one under a syllable. Each student will say his or her syllable in order. Those saying unstressed syllables will bend their knees as they say the sounds. Those saying stressed syllables will stand on their toes. Repeat the line several times until students can say it smoothly. Then have the class join in. Continue this activity with the remaining lines in the passage.

Redistribute the chunks of text at random. Then have students read their lines as before, this time rising to indicate stressed syllables and bending to indicate unstressed syllables.

Collect the phrases again. Ask students to write down whatever parts of text they can remember. What phrases or words stick in their mind?

Distribute copies of the full passage. By this time, the words will be very familiar. Lead the class in a group recitation of the passage (bending and rising as before or clapping to the rhythm). Solicit students' impressions of the words. What is this passage about? What unusual wordings, repe-

titions, or interesting patterns do they notice? Is it an upbeat or a sad speech? What other emotions came through?

As a creative finale, ask a few student volunteers to act out the speech from memory, with perhaps a prop or two for dramatic effect.

MORE TO DO

Advanced Rhythm: Besides the iamb (da DA), introduce students to its reverse rhythm, the trochee (DA da), and to the dactyl (DA da da) and its reverse rhythm, the anapest (da da DA). The names are less important than the ability to recognize these rhythms in poetry.

Have students classify their names or the names of famous people:

Iamb: Sir Paul, Queen Anne, Louise, Macbeth

Trochee: David, Oprah, Clara, Rosa, Robin

Dactyl: Helena, Frederick, Celia, Rosalind, Angelo, Mortimer, Romeo

Anapest: Anne Marie, Juliette, Earl of Kent, Mr. Spock

You're Order Out Of

Finding the subject of an inverted sentence.

PURPOSE

Help students recognize Shakespeare's inverted sentence structure—and reinforce their knowledge of grammar basics—by having them reorder and rearrange sentences to correctly identify the subject, object, and verb.

BACKGROUND INFORMATION

Shakespeare's frequent sentence inversions, in which the subject, verb, and object are out of their usual order, can sometimes trip up students. Shakespeare used this technique to shift the emphasis from one word to another and, less importantly, to conform to meter. For example, in the passage on Who's Got the Rhythm? (page 20) Romeo says "This love feel I" instead of "This love I feel" or "I feel this love." Say each phrase aloud. This first one stresses that he, Romeo, is the one who feels love, whereas the second

one emphasizes the word "feel."

WHAT TO DO

Ask students to think about how the speech of Shakespeare's characters differs from the way we talk. What is unfamiliar about the language? About the words or the sentences? Among other departures (such as the fact that people don't normally speak to each other in poetry) are word inversions. Why do students think that Shakespeare changed the word order?

Next, ask students to identify the subject, object, and verb in the following non-inverted line of iambic pentameter from *All's Well That Ends Well* (4.4.13):

You never had a servant to whose trust
Your business was more welcome.

Read the lines aloud. Then switch the order of some of the words and read the sentence again:

A servant you never had to whose trust
More welcome was your business.

Ask students if the sentence still makes sense. Does it have the same meaning as it did before? Can students pick out the subject (you), verb (had), and direct object (servant)? Point out that just because these words are in a new position doesn't necessarily mean they become new parts of speech.

If you've been studying rhythm, have the class read the uninverted and inverted sentences aloud to hear the difference. Explain that Shakespeare often changed the word order to emphasize a word or a feeling. Introduce students to several examples of inverted lines and practice putting the words in the correct order. Here are three examples from *Twelfth Night* (3.4.357–74):

> For him I imitate . . .
> For I imitate him . . .
>
> He named Sebastian; I my brother know
> He named Sebastian; I know my brother
>
> But, O, how vile an idol proves this god!
> But, O, this god proves how vile an idol!

Next have students complete the reproducible on page 21, which includes more inversions from various plays. Students can reorder them as they did the examples.

For greater challenge, divide the class into groups of four or five. For each group, make a copy of the reproducible, cut out each word from the different phrases (one word per paper), and put them in a baggie. (To simplify the exercise, number each piece of paper to identify which sentence the word came from.)

Ask students to arrange and rearrange the words into sentences. If students end up with six sentences that make sense—even if they're not the original text—then mission accomplished.

MORE TO DO

La Camisa Roja: Other languages often have word inversions (inversions to us, that is). For example, Spanish, French, and Italian speakers all generally put the adjective after the noun that it modifies, not before. "La camisa roja" is Spanish for "the shirt red." If you have any bilingual students in your classroom, ask them to share examples of word inversions in their native tongue. What parts of English word order do they find difficult?

Thine or Mine?: A stumbling block to reading Shakespeare is the archaic second-person pronouns (thee, thy, thine). These pronouns apply to familiar or inferior people—a woman talking to her dog, two children talking to each other, a king talking to a commoner.

Have students memorize this sentence:

Thou givest thee thine twine.

It means: You (singular) give (a different) you your twine. *Thou* is always a subject. *Thee* is an object. *Thine* and *mine* (yours and my) are possessive. The model sentence serves as a reminder.

Most verbs that agree with *thou* end in *-est* or *-st*: thou livest, canst, wouldst, didst, bring'st. Common irregular verbs include: thou art (are), dost (do), hast (have), shalt (shall), and wilt (will). Ask students to search for examples of these forms in a selected passage.

Answers to Reproducible

1. . . . were **he** not called Romeo; 2. **madness** must not go unwatched in great ones; 3. Our **remedies** oft lie in ourselves; 4. Let **gentleness** be my strong enforcement; 5. **Every one** doth swear to these injunctions; 6. When I beguile a fat, and bean-fed horse . . . And sometimes **I** lurk in a gossip's bowl.

Metaphorically Speaking

Unlocking the meaning of Shakespeare's metaphors.

PURPOSE

Develop students' understanding of figurative language by asking them to interpret, extend, and create metaphors.

BACKGROUND INFORMATION

A metaphor is a figure of speech in which an object is described by comparing it to something else. For example, in *A Midsummer Night's Dream*, a rose takes on special meaning as a metaphor for a woman's marital status. A rose plucked and distilled into perfume describes a married woman, while a rose that withers on the stem describes a spinster.

Shakespeare also used metaphors to describe more abstract topics such as life, time, and the meaning of the universe. In *The Tempest* and *A Midsummer Night's Dream*, life is a dream in which we can never be sure of what's real and what isn't. Prospero believes that the world will one day disappear into thin air, just as dreams do (4.1.156). In *As You Like It* (3.2.310), Rosalind compares time to the paces of a horse: "Time travels in divers paces with divers persons . . . I'll tell you who Time ambles withal, who Time trots withal, who Time gallops withal, and who he stands tall withal." In other words, though time is a constant, it seems to move faster or slower to different people.

Shakespeare's plays are rich in original metaphors, especially those relating to animals (birds in particular), war, fencing, hunting, fishing, music, food, clothing, and other familiar Elizabethan pastimes. Shakespeare was a country boy, and so his metaphors often conjure up natural and pastoral images.

All the World's a Stage

WHAT TO DO

To introduce the concept of metaphor and demonstrate Shakespeare's use of them, it's helpful to take a closer look at several examples. Start by reading aloud the following passage from *Much Ado About Nothing*:

> The pleasant'st angling is to see the fish
> Cut with her golden oars the silver stream,
> And greedily devour the treacherous bait;
> So we angle for Beatrice . . . (3.1.26)

The "fish" is Beatrice and the "bait" is false gossip that the hated Benedick actually loves Beatrice. Ursula and Hero (the "anglers") allow Beatrice to overhear this false gossip on purpose. Beatrice takes their bait "hook, line, and sinker"—she truly believes that Benedick loves her.

After reading the passage aloud, invite students to identify the metaphorical topic (fishing) and what it is being used to describe (tricking Beatrice). Then brainstorm and list words associated with the metaphor (angler, stream, river, lure, reel in, cast, pole, bait, worm, fly, hook, line, sinker, fish such as trout and bass, catch). Using the class-generated list, extend the metaphor: To lure a trout, you must use the right bait. Once you hook your catch, you can reel it in, and so on.

Next, have students work with the metaphors on the Metaphorically Speaking reproducible on pages 22 and 23.

To wrap up your metaphor lesson, have each student choose a new metaphorical topic (sports, plants, rocks, the stars, machines, animals) and apply it to the topic of school. To spark creative thinking, ask students questions such as "If this school were an animal, what animal would it be and why?" Have students list three things that school has in common with their topic. Here's an example for a turtle: 1. School days and turtles advance slowly. 2. They send their "young" into the world to take care of themselves. 3. Like a turtle's shell, the school walls protect the vulnerable contents.

MORE TO DO

More Metaphors: Spotting metaphors in the text can become an on-going game for students. Ask students to keep a running list of examples they find as they read. Once you've completed the play, students can compare metaphors and classify them by topic. The topics that Shakespeare chose give a glimpse into popular events and objects of the day. For example, war and hunting were much more common. The sea and sailing were as vital as automobiles and airplanes today. The stars and planets loomed ominously. Other categories include the skilled trades (carpentry, butchery, sewing, weaving), clothes, food and drink, jewels and precious metals, prisons, disease, sports, money, nature, and weather.

Similarly Speaking: Similes are usually easier for students to understand and write than metaphors. Similes compare one object with another using the words "like" or "as." A few examples:

I found him under a tree, like a dropped acorn. (*As You Like It* 3.2.235)

It seems she hangs upon the cheek of night As a rich jewel in an Ethiop's ear. (*Romeo and Juliet* 1.4.47)

Let's carve him as a dish fit for the gods, Not hew him as a carcass fit for hounds. (*Julius Caesar* 2.1.173)

A simple exercise is to ask each student to write the first half of a simile and then pass it to the next student to complete. For an extra challenge, students can continue passing the page to create several versions of the simile.

Rude Dude or Kind Mind?

Turn Shakespeare's most fiendish insults into clever compliments.

PURPOSE

While there's no question that insults—even 400-year-old ones—are not nice; understanding, rewriting, and writing insults can entice students into looking up difficult vocabulary words and expressing themselves on more sophisticated levels. That's right—low-down put-downs can carry students to a higher plane.

BACKGROUND INFORMATION

"Capping" is a modern slang term for trading clever insults back and forth. Students may be surprised to find that Shakespeare perfected this linguistic art form 400 years ago, and his insults are sure to capture your students' interest and imagination. His characters fling insults at one another and exchange clever and creative barbs in all the plays.

WHAT TO DO

This activity can be a positive experience if you focus on the language and challenge students to turn all the insults into compliments. The following be-all and end-all of Shakespearean insults is an excellent example of creative use of words. Kent, a banished earl in King Lear's court, is picking a fight with Oswald, the steward of Lear's daughter, Goneril:

A knave, a rascal, and eater of broken meats [scraps of food, as a beggar would eat]; a base, proud, shallow, beggarly, three-suited [servants had only three suits], hundred-pound [not rich], filthy worsted-stocking [clothes a servant would wear] knave; a lily-livered, action-taking [not a fighter], whoreson, glass-gazing [vain and conceited], superserviceable [unprincipled], finical [over fastidious] rogue; one trunk-inheriting slave; one that . . . art nothing but the composition [compound or material] of a knave, beggar, coward, pander . . . *King Lear* 2.2.14

Dissect this speech with your students. After reading the passage and defining the words, ask students to analyze the choice of words. What expressions are surprising or poetic? For example, an "eater of broken meats" describes a beggar in an indirect way. A "glass-gazing" person is someone who's always looking in a mirror.

What aspect of Oswald does Kent attack most fiercely? How many words are class-related? What types of things distinguish Oswald's class from the nobility, according to Kent?

Based on Kent's diatribe, has Oswald done anything to merit this attack? Is being poor, vain, or unfashionably clothed grounds for insult? What personality traits does Kent apply to Oswald?

Kent draws his sword, but the frightened Oswald screams for help rather than fight. What would students do if faced with such an unexpected attack? What would they say? What words would describe an earl in negative terms?

Divide students into groups of three or four and distribute the reproducible on page 24. Have groups decipher and respond to the insults listed and then turn the insults into clever compliments.

Students can draw inspiration from the insult quoted above and examples they've come across in the play you're reading. Emphasize that both creativity and an ability to imitate Shakespearean language are important.

MORE TO DO

'Invent a Word': A modern, well-educated, English-language writer uses roughly 10,000 different words—total—in a lifetime. Shakespeare used between 18,000 and 21,000 in his plays and sonnets. Many of those words he invented to suit his own dramatic or poetic purposes—such as creating clever insults. A sampling of his contributions to English language: assassination, dislocate, eyesore, hoodwinked, premeditated, reliance, submerged, and tongue-tied.

Students can experiment with language and vocabulary by creating a clever name for a new product—a car, a stereo, or an article of clothing. Brainstorm a list of nouns related to the product and a separate list of adjectives. For a car, students might list wheel, auto, steel, zoomer, fast, corner-turning, safe, rugged, and so on. Students might want to look at magazines and advertisements for inspiration.

Write the words on separate sheets of paper and drop them into two bags—one for nouns and one for adjectives. Challenge students to each select one word from each bag to create a catchy, creative name. They can continue mixing different combinations of nouns and adjectives until they find something they like.

Modern Shakespeare

Students put Shakespeare in their own words.

PURPOSE

Students translate famous passages into modern language. But first they have to figure out what the passages mean.

WHAT TO DO

Begin by reading the following famous speech from *As You Like It*, to your class.

> All the world's a stage,
> And all the men and women merely players;
> They have their exits and their entrances,
> And one man in his time plays many parts,
> His acts being seven ages. At first, the infant,
> Mewling and puking in the nurse's arms,

> Then the whining schoolboy with his satchel,
> And shining morning face, creeping like a snail
> Unwillingly to school. And then the lover,
> Sighing like a furnace, with a woeful ballad
> Made to his mistress' eyebrow. Then a soldier
> Full of strange oaths and bearded like the pard
> Jealous in honor, sudden and quick in quarrel,
> Seeking the bubble reputation
> Even in the cannon's mouth. And then the justice,
> In fair round belly with good capon lined,
> With eyes severe and beard of formal cut,
> Full of wise saws and modern instances;

And so he plays his part. The sixth ages
    shifts
Into the lean and slippered pantaloon,
With spectacles on nose and pouch on side;
His youthful hose, well saved, a world too
    wide
For his shrunk sank, and his big manly
    voice,
Turning again his childish treble, pipes
And whistles in his sound. Last scene of all,
That ends this strange eventful history,
Is second childishness and mere oblivion,
Sans teeth, sans eyes, sans taste, sans
    everything.

(As You Like It 2.7.138)

After you've read it, ask students: What type of character might be speaking (man, woman, old, young, etc.)? What's the main message? Can students paraphrase it in their own words? (The speech is the melancholy character Jaques' view of life.)

Next, divide students into groups of three or four and give each group a copy of the reproducible on page 25 to translate. In addition to the passage on the reproducible, you can select passages from the play you're reading or allow each group to choose their own passage. Give each group a dictionary, but let students decipher the meaning of the passage themselves. They don't have to understand every word or nuance; they just have to make enough sense of it to accurately translate the gist of it.

Collect the translations and read them aloud. Compare the different versions and as a class, discuss the main point of the speech. If groups are translating passages from the play you're reading in class, challenge students to find or guess other groups' original passages based on the translations.

MORE TO DO

Boy Meets Girl: Having students paraphrase a story or retell it in their own words is an excellent way to help them focus on the main idea. For example, how would students sum up the play you are reading in one sentence? Can they do it in five words or less? *A Midsummer Night's Dream* could be described as "Fairies mess up lovers' lives—or is it just a dream?" Even shorter: "Life is a dream—isn't it?"

A fun game to help students summarize the "main idea" is to challenge them to describe fairy tales or popular movies in fewer and fewer words. Begin by asking a volunteer to retell the basic plot from beginning to end. Then have students describe the same plot in writing, using five sentences or less. Read a few descriptions aloud. Then challenge students to sum up the whole fairy tale or movie in a sentence.

Finally, working together as a class, find a way to express the main theme in five words or less. *Romeo and Juliet* could be described in several ways: "Hate kills." "True love is forever." "No one escapes fate." "Love thy neighbor."

Humorous Homonyms and Other Puns

A lesson on puns and word play.

PURPOSE

Capitalize on students' love of a good play on words to bring them closer to the text and give them a deeper appreciation of Shakespeare's gift for language.

BACKGROUND INFORMATION

Shakespeare's plays are filled with puns. One scholar counted 114 puns in Macbeth alone! Shakespeare often used substitution to create puns spoken by clowns or bumbling, peasant-class characters or characters who are trying (but failing) to put on airs. Nobles use substitution more deliberately. For example, Macbeth says, "This push/Will <u>cheer</u> me ever or <u>disseat</u> me now." (5.3.22). *Cheer* is a pun on *chair*, as in *throne*. *Disseat* means "dethrone."

Two other types of pun, used more often by noble characters, rely on homonyms (pail pale) or double meanings (rail meaning "banister" or "complain").

Not all of Shakespeare's puns are still clear or funny. Some original meanings of words, and thus the jokes, have changed or been lost over time. For other puns, many seemingly innocent words had dual connotations of a sexual nature in Elizabethan times.

The puns that have survived are the focus of this activity. There are more than enough to go around.

WHAT TO DO

Write on the board: "Puns are a low form of humor, but I think poetry is verse." This pun relies on substituting a similar-sounding word with a different meaning. Ask students: What word creates the pun? (*verse*) What word does it replace? (*worse*) What does the sentence mean? Does it make sense?

After introducing students to the three types of puns that Shakespeare used—substitution, homonyms, and double meanings—distribute the reproducible on page 26. Allow them to use a dictionary or thesaurus to research the words as they complete the activity.

Reveal the answers (on the following page), and discuss how and why Shakespeare uses puns in the play you're reading. Which characters utter the most puns? Why did Shakespeare choose these characters to be punny? What is the effect of the puns on other characters? On the audience? Ask students to keep a running list of puns as they read the play; many are cited and explained in the textual notes.

The obvious effect of puns is humor—making people laugh—but look for situations in which other issues are at stake:

* Two strong-headed rivals one-up each other with cleverness. Benedick and Beatrice verbally spar in several places in *Much Ado About Nothing,* including 1.1.110, 2.3.242, and 5.2.42. Katherine and Petruchio heat up the stage in *The Taming of the Shrew* (2.1.185 and 4.5.1).

- One character uses puns to insult another. Rosalind and Touchstone hurl insults in *As You Like It* (1.2.56). Anne spits verbal venom at Richard III in the second scene of the play. Many others follow suit in later scenes, especially Queen Elizabeth (4.4.195). The four lovers in *A Midsummer Night's Dream* call each other names after falling under the influence of Puck's potion (3.2.180).

- A lower-class character befuddles a higher-class one. The cobbler baffles Marcellus in *Julius Caesar* (1.1.1). The gravedigger engages in word play with Hamlet (5.1.120).

Encourage students to collect and share puns that they encounter day-to-day. Look for puns in newspaper and magazine headlines, advertisements, jokes, and so on.

MORE TO DO

Not-So-Well-Spoken: Much of Shakespeare's humor revolves around bumbling, peasant-class "clowns." Besides physical humor, they utter hilarious malapropisms—the wrong words in the right places. The malapropisms generally mean the opposite of what the speaker intends, and they're not always legitimate words.

Constable Dogberry in *Much Ado About Nothing* is a classic example (3.2.1, 3.5.1, 4.2.1, and 5.1.205). He calls his colleague a desartless man (instead of "deserving"), a senseless and fit man (instead of "sensible"), and someone who will comprehend all vagrom men (instead of "apprehend" and "vagrant").

Students will enjoy creating their own malapropisms—a vocabulary exercise in definitions and antonyms. Give students a list of eight to ten words that lend them-

selves to corruption, such as succeed, recede, delegate, idol, adamant, generate, constable, vigilant, concern, odious, tedious, suspicious, and so on. Have them work in small groups to "corrupt" six or eight of the words in Dogberry's vein and use their malapropisms in sentences. For example: Michael Jordan is an idle to many people.

Answers to Reproducible

I. 1. sun (Claudius and Gertrude complained that Hamlet was spending too much time in dark shadows; Hamlet's response refers to his unwanted status as stepson to Claudius); 2. souls (the cobbler says it's a trade he can use with "safe conscience"); 3. mettle (Beatrice is complaining of the inadequacies of men); 4. tale (A clown is referring to the tail on a musical instrument; the musician thinks he's talking about a story)

II. 1. musical note and written note (the musician is also making a pun on "noting," which was pronounced just like "nothing"); 2. stature and stench (Touchstone means the former, but Rosalind deliberately interprets it as the latter); 3. serious and dead (Mercutio is dying after a street fight); 4. appendages and weapons (the gravedigger means Adam had the first arms for digging, but his coworker thinks he means weapons); 5. falsehood (drink made him believe in illusions) and prone position (it put him to sleep); 6. variety or female-male distinction

The Great Shakespeare Word Quest

A scavenger hunt for examples of literary devices.

PURPOSE

Students can put their knowledge of word play, metaphors, similes, and other literary devices to the test with the Great Shakespeare Word Quest.

WHAT TO DO

Once students understand the basics of word play, metaphors, similes, and other literary devices, they are ready to put their knowledge to the test with The Great Shakespeare Word Quest (page 27). Add a few play-specific items to the list (items 13, 14, and 15 on page 27). For example, you could ask students to find the first time a character declares his or her love for someone, a few lines that sum up a major message in the play, or a turning point in the plot. Have students work in pairs or small groups to search for all the items. The quest can take place over a few days, while you're reading the play, or you can make it a post-reading activity.

As in any great quest, there's a prize for those who succeed. Round up something appropriate to the era or the play, such as "Renaissance" (butterscotch) candies, strawberries (for *Othello* or *Richard III*), wildflowers or wildflower stickers (for *Romeo and Juliet, Hamlet,* and *King Lear*), and so on.

MORE TO DO

Motif Scavenger Hunt: A motif is an image or idea that is repeated throughout a play. Examples of motifs include: ears in *Hamlet,* eyes and sight in *King Lear*, blood in *Macbeth*, dreams or a dreamlike state in *A Midsummer Night's Dream,* masks or disguises in *Much Ado About Nothing,* books or learning in *The Tempest.*

As you read the text, encourage students to identify examples of a motif. Keep a running list. At the end of the play, examine and compare the items: How many examples are direct mentions and how many are indirect mentions? How many examples are metaphors? Parts of songs? Which character or characters are most associated with the motif? Why did Shakespeare use motifs in his plays?

Who's Got the Rhythm?

Romeo's lament is an example of blank verse. The basic rhythm is da DA da DA da DA da DA da DA. But at the beginning of lines 2 and 6, Shakespeare alters this rhythm. In doing so, he brings attention to the words "why" and "feather."

In line 4, saying the word "serious" in two syllables instead of three ("SEER yus") keeps the rhythm on track.

1 Here's **much** to **do** with **hate**, \ but **more** with **love.**

2 **Why** then, \ O **brawl**ing *love*, \ O *lov*ing **hate**,

3 O **anything** \ of **noth**ing **first** cre**ate**;

4 O **heav**y **light**ness, \ **ser**ious **van**ity,

5 Mis**shape**n **cha**os \ **of** well-**seem**ing **forms**,

6 **Feath**er of **lead**, \ bright **smoke**, cold **fire**, \ sick **health**,

7 Still-**wak**ing **sleep** \ that **is** not **what** it **is!**

8 This **love** feel **I**, \ that **feel** no **love** in **this**.

(Romeo and Juliet 1.1.172)

Notes:
  3 "of nothing first create": created out of nothing in the first place.
  5 "well-seeming": seemingly beautiful
  7 "still-waking": always awake
  8 "feel no love in this": doesn't love in return

You're Order Out Of

Read each inverted sentence. Circle the subject. Then rewrite the sentence using standard English word order (noun, verb, object). How does the meaning of the sentence change?

1. So Romeo would, were he not Romeo called,

   Retain that dear perfection which he owes . . .

   _____

   (*Romeo and Juliet* 2.2.45)

2. Madness in great ones must not unwatched go.

   _____

   (*Hamlet* 3.1.131)

3. Our remedies oft in ourselves do lie.

   _____

   (*All's Well That Ends Well* 1.1.220)

4. Let gentleness my strong enforcement be . . .

   _____

   (*As You Like It* 2.7.118)

5. To these injunctions every one doth swear . . .

   _____

   (*The Merchant of Venice* 2.9.18)

6. When I a fat, and bean-fed horse beguile . . .

   And sometimes lurk I in a gossip's bowl.

   _____

   (*A Midsummer Night's Dream* 2.1.45)

Metaphorically Speaking

Try your hand at interpreting the metaphors below. Then create a few of your own.

METAPHOR 1: The Meaning of Macbeth

Here are two short metaphors from the first act of *Macbeth*. For each one, write two or three sentences in your own words to describe what the metaphor means.

> If you can look into the seeds of time,
> And say which grain will grow and which will not,
> Speak then to me . . .
>> (*Macbeth* 1.3.58)

_____

_____

> [Duncan to Macbeth] Welcome hither.
> I have begun to plant thee, and will labor
> To make thee full of growing.
>> (*Macbeth* 1.4.27)

_____

_____

METAPHOR 2: Hamlet's Troubles

This famous speech from *Hamlet* includes a military metaphor. The "slings and arrows" are problems that fate keeps flinging at Hamlet. The question is, should Hamlet just suffer these slings and arrows or take up his own weapons to end them?

> To be, or not to be; that is the question:
> Whether 'tis nobler in the mind to suffer
> The slings and arrows of outrageous fortune,
> Or to take arms against a sea of troubles,
> And, by opposing, end them.
> (*Hamlet*, 3.1.58)

TEACHING SHAKESPEARE—YES YOU CAN! • THE PLAY'S THE THING
Scholastic Professional Books, 1998

Apply the military metaphor to your own "sea of troubles." In what ways do these troubles "wound" you? What kind of weapons best describe their pain? What metaphoric weapons do you have? Use as many military terms as you can to describe how you could fight these troubles including; gun, cannon, armor, helmet, soldier, battle, army, uniform, battalion, fife, and drum.

_____

_____

_____

_____

METAPHOR 3: All the World's a Spacesh

"All the world's a stage" are famous words in a famous metaphor. We live on a stage. We're sim ply actors, playing many parts during our lifetimes. Read the passage below. Then rewrite it with a new metaphor: "All the world's a spaceship." Use space-related words such as "lift-off" to describe the "seven ages" of humans from birth to death.

> All the world's a stage,
> And all the men and women merely players.
> They have their exits and their entrances,
> And one man in his time plays many parts,
> His acts being seven ages.

(*As You Like It* 2.7.138)

_____

_____

_____

_____

_____

Rude Dude or Kind Mind?

For each insult, write a witty retort (comeback) on a separate sheet of paper. Imitate Shakespeare's language as best you can. Then rewrite the insult to make it a clever compliment.

1. More of your conversation would infect my brain. (*Coriolanus* 2.1.93)

2. You cram these words into mine ears against the stomach of my sense. (*The Tempest* 2.1.102)

3. What a wretched and peevish fellow is he, to mope with his fat-brained followers so far out of his knowledge! (*Henry V* 3.7.133)

4. Mend my company, take away thyself. (*Timon of Athens* 4.3.285)

5. You juggler! You canker blossom! You thief of love! (*A Midsummer Night's Dream* 3.2.282)

6. Get you gone, you dwarf/You minimus, of hind'ring knotgrass made/You bead, you acorn! (*A Midsummer Night's Dream* 3.2.328)

7. [You have an] undressed, unpolished, uneducated, unpruned, untrained, or rather unlettered, or ratherest, unconfirmed fashion. (*Love's Labour's Lost* 4.2.16)

8. Foul wrinkled witch, what mak'st thou in my sight? (*Richard III* 1.3.164)

For an extra challenge, rewrite this insult:

[You are] scambling, outfacing, fashion-monging boys,
That lie, and cog, and flout, deprave, and slander,
Go anticly, and show outward hideousness,
And speak off half a dozen dang'rous words,
How [you] might hurt [your] enemies, if [you] durst,
And this is all. (*Much Ado About Nothing* 5.1.94)

TEACHING SHAKESPEARE—YES YOU CAN! • THE PLAY'S THE THING
Scholastic Professional Books, 1998

Modern Shakespeare

The following speech is from the play *Julius Caesar*. It is Mark Antony's eulogy at Julius Caesar's funeral. Read the speech and translate it into modern English.

Friends, Romans, countrymen, lend me your ears;
I come to bury Caesar, not to praise him.
The evil that men do lives after them,
The good is oft interred with their bones;
So let it be with Caesar. The noble Brutus
Hath told you Caesar was ambitious
If it were so, it was a grievous fault,
And grievously hath Caesar answered it.
Here, under leave of Brutus and the rest
(For Brutus is an honorable man,
So are they all, all honorable men)
Come I to speak in Caesar's funeral.
He was my friend, faithful and just to me;
But Brutus says he was ambitious,
And Brutus is an honorable man.
He hath brought many captives home to Rome,
Whose ransoms did the general coffers fill.
Did this in Caesar seem ambitious?

When that the poor have cried, Caesar hath wept.
Ambition should be made of sterner stuff.
Yet Brutus says he was ambitious;
And Brutus is an honorable man.
You all did see that on the Lupercal
I thrice presented him a kingly crown,
Which he did thrice refuse. Was this ambition?
Yet Brutus says he was ambitious;
And sure he is an honorable man.
I speak not to disprove what Brutus spoke,
But I am here to speak what I do know.
You all did love him once, not without cause;
What cause withholds you then to mourn for him?
O judgement! Thou art fled to brutish beasts,
And men have lost their reason. Bear with me;
My heart is in the coffin there with Caesar,
And I must pause till it come back to me.

(Julius Caesar 3.2.76)

Humorous Homonyms and Other Puns

I. Fill in the blank with a homonym for the underlined word. A homonym is a word that sounds like another word but has a different spelling and meaning: die and dye. Shakespeare used homonyms to make puns.

1. I am too much in the 'son.' _____ (*Hamlet* 1.2.67)

2. I am but as you would say a cobbler . . . a mender of bad soles. _____
(*Julius Caesar* 1.1.11)

3. Not til God make men of some other metal than earth. _____
(*Much Ado About Nothing* 2.1.51)

4. Thereby hangs a tail. _____ (*Othello* 3.1.8)

II. Some words have more than one meaning: leaves can mean "departs" or "foliage on trees." Double meanings make great puns. For each line, write two meanings of the underlined word or words.

1. There's not a note of mine that's worth the noting. (*Much Ado About Nothing* 2.3.53)

_____

2. Touchstone   Nay, if I keep not my rank —
    Rosalind   Thou losest thy old smell. (*As You Like It* 1.2.100)

_____

3. Ask for me tomorrow, and you shall find me a grave man.
(*Romeo and Juliet* 3.1.98)

_____

4. A' (Adam) was the first that ever bore arms. (*Hamlet* 5.1.33)

_____

5. I believe drink gave thee the lie last night. (*Macbeth* 2.3.37)

_____

6. Our bodies are gardens, to the which our wills are gardeners . . . supply it
with one gender of herbs or distract it with many . . . (*Othello* 1.3.320)

_____

Name_____ Date_____

The Great Shakespeare Word Quest

Your quest is a difficult but honorable one: Search the play for each of these valuable items. Write down your findings and their locations (act, scene, line number).

1. A rhymed couplet that ends a scene. _____

2. Three words contracted into one. _____

3. An Elizabethan word no longer in use. _____

4. A pun or other joke. _____

5. A metaphor or simile. _____

6. A clever insult. _____

7. A sentence inversion. _____

8. A great phrase that we still use today. _____

9. A reference to each sense (sight, sound, smell, taste, touch).

_____

10. Two lines that echo each other (spoken by different characters).

_____

11. A malapropism (misspoken word designed for comic effect).

_____

12. A word that has a double meaning._____

13. _____

14. _____

15. _____

More Activity Ideas: Mirth and Merriment

Continue to explore Shakespeare's language with motivating games and humorous exercises.

A Humorous ~~Humorless~~ Joke

Act 2, scene 3 of *Macbeth* is the spawning ground of the Knock-Knock joke. Someone keeps knocking on the door of a drunken porter. He repeats, "Knock, knock, who's there?" several times, fearing that the answer might be the devil, but doesn't get a reply.

Here's a chance for students to share a few of their own "Knock Knock Jokes" in direct imitation of Shakespeare!

Know Exaggeration

Shakespeare taps into our sense of the absurd when he makes a humorous point through exaggeration. For example, in Act 2 scene 1 of *Much Ado About Nothing,* Benedick tries to avoid talking to Beatrice by asking the prince to send him on an errand. His requests are off the wall: "I will fetch you a tooth-picker now from the furthest inch of Asia; bring you the length of Prester John's foot; fetch you a hair off the great Cham's beard . . ."

Using this example or a similar one taken from the text you're studying, have students play "Who Can Top This?" Students can work in small groups. challenge them to come up with similar exaggerations or to modernize Shakespeare's examples. What could Benedick bring his

Prince today? Golf balls from the moon? A hair from Michael Jordan's head? Two identical snowflakes?

Vocabulary Lotto Game: To reinforce vocabulary words (see the Mini-Glossary on page 79), construct a simple Lotto game. Make a deck of 30 to 40 definitions (one per card) and a corresponding deck of vocabulary words. Give each student a board with nine squares (3 x 3) and nine different vocabulary cards. (It's okay for two students to have some of the same words.) Students place these cards face-up on their boards, covering every square.

To begin, select definitions at random from the deck and read them aloud. Any students who have the matching vocabulary card can turn it over. As in Bingo, the object is to be the first one to turn over three cards in a row—up, down, across, or diagonally. Students say "Lotto!" to signal that they have copleted a line.

Will-Spoken

Using the Poster in Your Classroom

Famous Phrases

(language arts)

Before hanging the poster in your classroom, try playing a game of 20 questions using phrases from the poster. Tell students that you're going to read them a selection of phrases and their mission is to guess what the phrases have in common. Read aloud each of the expressions from the poster, pausing after every three or four selections to allow students to ask questions. After you have revealed the source—or students have guessed it—display the poster and discuss the meaning of each phrase with students. (See Will-Spoken Glossary on page 31.)

Picture Puns

(language arts, fine arts)

Shakespeare used both verbal and visual puns. For example, in the hilarious act 2 Scene 2 of *The Tempest*, the drunken Stephano stumbles on "a monster with four legs and two voices." In fact, the audience sees that the "monster" is really two people—Caliban and Trinculo—hiding under a cloth with only their legs showing.

Using the poster as inspiration, have students isolate favorite lines and pair them with visuals—either their own illustrations or photos from old magazines and catalogues—to make puns. The ripest lines to pick are those with words or ideas that can mean more than one thing. Here are a few examples:

* "Friends, Romans, countrymen, lend me your ears" (*Julius Caesar*) paired with a picture of a family picnic with ears of corn

* "To be or not to be. That is the question" (*Hamlet*) as the caption for a confused postal worker in front of an array of mailboxes ("2B or not 2B")

* "What wouldst thou have, boor? what, thickskin? speak, breathe, discuss: brief short, quick, snap" (*The Merry Wives of Windsor*) as a thought bubble for a waiter serving a customer who can't decide

Shakespeare-Filled Dialogue

Challenge students to write a scene between two characters using at least five of the expressions from the poster. Students can pick the subject and the style of the piece—they just need to work ten phrases from the poster into the dialogue.

Go to the Source

Ask students to each pick one expression and find it in the original text. Have students write a brief description of where in the play it was used, who spoke the line, and in what context it was used.

Will-Spoken Display

During your Shakespeare unit, make the Will-Spoken poster the centerpiece of a Shakespeare Bulletin Board. As you study different aspects of Shakespeare's writing, add to the display. For example:

❀ Have students jot down any famous phrases or expressions they come across as they read. Post the expressions, with a brief definition, on the bulletin board.

❀ After completing the metaphor activities (page 12), keep a running list of metaphors you encounter in the text on the bulletin board. Also keep a tally of favorite puns and clever insults.

❀ Using the examples they found completing the Great Shakespeare Word Quest, have students design and illustrate their own mini Will-Spoken posters.

Will-Spoken Glossary

The expressions on the poster represent just a sampling of Shakespeare's contributions to the English language.

hoodwinked: tricked

my salad days: As Cleopatra describes it, her days as a naive youth, when she was "green in judgement, cold in blood"

all the world's a stage: we are all just actors playing roles; Shakespeare alludes to the world as a stage in several plays

neither rhyme nor reason: without logic or a plan

the primrose path of dalliance: easy living without care for duty or the future; a primrose is a delicate yellow-flowered herb

in my heart of hearts: my deepest, truest feelings

eat out of house and home: take advantage of hospitality

household words: words (or names) that everyone knows and uses

dead as a doornail: *really* dead, no question about it

the milk of human-kindness: Lady Macbeth's disdainful assessment of her husband as a person with a sweet and kind nature who is unable to do wrong or to do harm

the be-all and the end-all: the central, most important part

Knock! Knock! Who's there?: the first lines of a silly joke

full of sound and fury: a lot of noise with little meaning; also used in the title of a famous novel by William Faulkner, *The Sound and the Fury.*

what the dickens: what on earth; what in the world; "dickens" is another name for "devil" or "deuce"

laughing-stock: an object of ridicule; the butt of a joke

wear my heart on my sleeve: show feelings openly—often means a little too openly

pomp and circumstance: stately, elaborate ceremony; the name of a popular song played during graduations and other important events

green-eyed monster: jealousy; people also say "green with envy" but jealousy and envy are not synonymous; jealousy involves people and envy involves things

wild-goose chase: eager search for something that doesn't exist

a fool's paradise: a state of happiness based on false beliefs or hopes

to not budge an inch: to be stubborn; stick to one's guns

an eye-sore: something (or someone) ugly

melted into thin air: disappeared

laugh yourself into stitches: split your sides laughing hard

All the School's a Stage

Wherein players read, perform, and interpret the text.

Character Trading Cards

Make trading cards that feature a character's vital stats.

PURPOSE

Get students better acquainted with the cast of characters by creating character trading cards.

WHAT TO DO

To help keep track of the characters in the play, students can use the reproducible on page 43 to create character trading cards. Have students work together to make a card for each of the major characters in the play. Students can fill in the age (or approximate age), relatives, social class, and feats and foibles of each character. Make several sets of the cards and have them available for students

to refer to throughout the unit. You can use also use the cards for a variety of activities, including Who's Who at the Masked Ball?

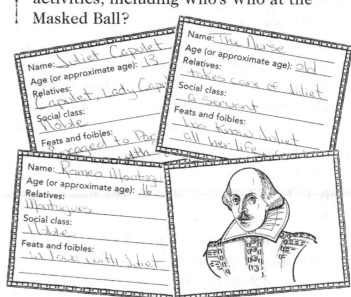

Who's Who at the Masked Ball?

A role-playing game in which everyone plays a character and tries to deduce who's playing whom by asking probing questions.

Purpose

How well do students know the Shakespeare characters they've met? In Who's Who at the Masked Ball students try to think and act like characters in the play.

What to Do

To play the Masked Ball game, clear a large, open space in the center of the room. Give each student a character trading card and, just for a fun, a mask. (Duplicate characters are not a problem.)

Announce one topic of conversation for the party—sports, movies, TV shows, music, or clothing. Allow students two or three minutes to think about their character in terms of this topic. As they play the game, students conceal their character's identity.

Let the ball begin! For five minutes, have students mill around, talking to as many people as they can about the chosen topic. No other topic is allowed, including the play or the names of the characters. The objective is to deduce as many identities as possible by asking probing questions. Here are some questions for the topic of sports: What sport do you like best? Do you play on the men's team or the women's team? Where do you usually go figure skating—at the castle rink or on a pond in the woods? Do you have plenty of money to buy all of that golf equipment?

The idea is to draw out the character's gender, station in life, attitudes, and personality. Students answer questions as

best they can. If they don't know an answer based on the information in the play, they just make it up! The only rule is that the answer must be in character. Here's how various characters might answer the same question:

> Questioner: What type of movies do you like?
>
> Romeo: Romantic love stories, especially when the guy gets the girl in the end.
>
> Juliet: Love stories starring handsome, young noblemen.
>
> Mercutio: Action adventure.

When time is up, ask students to guess and discuss who's who. Encourage them to state what fact led to their conclusions. Once a character is revealed, ask the role player to describe how he or she made the character relate to the chosen topic.

MORE TO DO

Similar as a Simile: If you were a weather system, what weather system would you be? Silly as this question might sound, it can direct students to the heart of understanding characters—their identities, motivations, and natures. Take Hamlet: His sometimes stormy, sometimes fragile psyche is like a thunderstorm that booms and abates. The mischievous Puck in *A Midsummer Night's Dream* is more like a surprise gust of wind that blows off a hat. Pose the above question to students and ask them to compare characters with different types of weather. Then students can turn their character comparisons into similes and metaphors (see page 12). Hamlet is like a thunderstorm out of control. Puck is as mischievous as a gust of wind in a feather factory.

The Man With Two Faces: Often, the characters in Shakespeare's plays will display a public and a private face. They act one way when they're with people and reveal different motives or feelings when they're alone. For example, Claudius (from *Hamlet*) is guilt-ridden, calculating, and a little paranoid when alone in his chamber or a chapel, but to other characters he appears the perfect statesman.

In her book *Shakespeare: A Teaching Guide* (J. Weston Walch; 1993), Sharon Hamilton describes a mime activity in which pairs of students portray the public and private faces of a character. Students work in pairs with one student representing the private face of the character and the other student representing the public face. The pairs then experiment together to find poses that represents the two sides of the characters. Then, standing back-to-back, they strike statuelike poses (with minimal movement) for the class to observe. For example, if students were portraying Claudius, one student could reflect Claudius as statesman by standing straight and tall while the other student portrays Claudius's guilt for covering his face. Afterward, actors discuss their new insights into the character, including his emotions and internal conflict.

Other two-faced characters could include the bastard son Don John (*Much Ado About Nothing*), the gender-bending Viola (*Twelfth Night*) and Rosalind (*As You Like It*), Puck (*A Midsummer Night's Dream*), the mad King Lear (who banishes and is banished), the murdering Macbeth, and the devious Iago (*Othello*).

Dying in Style

Delving into the meaning of a character's last words.

PURPOSE

Faking a dramatic death is not just for hams. It's a great way to entice students to focus on the meaning of key passages.

BACKGROUND INFORMATION

Characters who die onstage miraculously seem to hang around just long enough to give a key speech or disclose vital information. These "famous last words" often neatly sum up the motivations behind a character's action or the main themes of the drama.

The speeches don't have to be long: "Et tu, Brute" is all that Julius Caesar needs to say. These three little words sum up a change in character that drives the entire main plot—all the way to Brutus's guilt-ridden suicide at the end.

The speeches don't come only from the dying person: "Good night, sweet Prince" is Horatio's final tribute to his dead friend Hamlet, whose last act was to hand the kingdom of Denmark to Fortinbras.

While the major characters don't die in the comedies, the characters will often profess their views on life and death in speech. For example, the "All the World's a Stage" speech from *As You Like It*.

What to Do

Begin by introducing a short death speech from your play (see box on page 36). Read, define, and decipher the text. Then ask probing questions: In plain English, what is the main message of the speech? What does the speech reveal about the character? About other characters? Do the words foreshadow future events? Do they explain any past events? Do students notice anything unusual?

Next, have small groups of students read and discuss death scenes from the play you're reading or in the case of the comedies, scenes in which characters discuss death or the meaning of life. (See box for suggestions.) As they discuss the scene, students should think about an epitaph—a short phrase that would appear on the character's tombstone—that would be fitting for the character.

Next, it's time for the hams in your class to *really* ham it up. Have each group prepare a short, original scene about the death of the character. The scene should include the question, "What do you want on your tombstone?" The answer, of course, is the epitaph that students have created.

The chosen character doesn't have to die in the real play to become a focus of a group's scene. Students can concoct any likely death scenario befitting the person. Remind students that the actor has to be alive and talking to deliver the vital last lines. Students who prefer not to act can supply simple props, sound effects, or a brief narration to set the scene.

More to Do

A Grave Man: The foreshadowing of death throughout *Romeo and Juliet* runs from the ominous (Juliet: "My grave is like to be my wedding bed." 1.5.134) to the humorous (Mercutio: "Ask for me tomorrow and you shall find me a grave man." 3.1.98). Encourage interested students to search for, compile, and compare these references. Include mentions of the color black and death-related metaphors. Students can creatively display their discoveries on a poster, in a song, or in a rap.

Death's Door: Explore the theme of death in one or more Shakespeare plays. Working in groups, have students scour the text to tabulate the ways in which characters die. How many die naturally? How many are killed? How are they killed? Students can plot their data on a pie graph or bar graph.

Each student can select one interesting death and write a police statement from the point of view of a witness. What happened, blow by blow? What was he or she wearing? Where did the death take place? How did other characters respond to the death? Why was the manner of death just or unjust?

Dying Words of Interest

HAMLET: The third and fifth acts are rich with life-and-death musings, particularly Hamlet's famous "To be or not to be" (3.1.56) and "Alas, poor Yorick" (5.1.188) speeches. For last dying words, Gertrude finally wakes up to reality and tips off Hamlet to her husband's and Hamlet's uncle's treachery (5.2.310). Fatally poisoned, Laertes and Hamlet bury the hatchet, so to speak (5.2.315).

KING LEAR: The evil Edmund has a change of character and does his first and last good deed just before he dies. (5.4.162).

RICHARD III: The evil king dies a just death (5.4.6) after the ghosts of his numerous murder victims have haunted him.

ROMEO AND JULIET: Mercutio receives a fatal sword wound but lives long enough to utter a couple of puns and curse both family houses (3.1.97). Juliet's pseudo-death speech (4.1.15) is more interesting than her real one (5.3.161) because she genuinely fears dying and has more time to think about it.

JULIUS CAESAR: Cassius, Brutus, and Titanius commit suicide, bathed in guilt and remorse.

Cassius: O, coward that I am to live so long
To see my best friend ta'en before my face! (5.3.35)

Titanius: By your leave, gods: This is a Roman part: Come, Cassius's sword, and find Titanius's heart. (5.3.88)

Brutus: Caesar, now be still:
I killed not thee with half so good a will.(5.5.50)

MACBETH: Macbeth repeats the final words of his first murder victims to his wife, and Shakespeare chose them for maximum guilt: "Murder!" "God bless us!" "Amen!" Also consider Macbeth's famous speech after he hears of his wife's death (5.3.24):

Life's but a walking shadow, a poor player
That struts and frets his hour upon the stage,
And then is heard no more; it is a tale
Told by an idiot, full of sound and fury,
Signifying nothing.

Although the only main characters who die are those in histories and tragedies, don't overlook comedies. Students can decipher speeches about death and the meaning of life. Five examples follow:

AS YOU LIKE IT: After meeting the Fool in the forest, Jacques mutters clever lines of despair (2.7.25):

And so from hour to hour we ripe, and ripe
And then from hour to hour we rot and rot;
And thereby hangs a tale.

THE TEMPEST: Prospero ends *The Tempest* with his famous "life is but a dream" speech (4.1.157):

We are such stuff
As dreams are made on; and our little life
Is rounded with a sleep.

MUCH ADO ABOUT NOTHING: Hero's fake epitaph (5.3.3) recounts the injustice done against her and makes Claudio feel even more like a villain.

MEASURE FOR MEASURE: The imprisoned Claudio begs his sister to save him from execution (3.1.117).

TWELFTH NIGHT: Olivia and Feste talk about death (1.5.54).

TEACHING SHAKESPEARE—YES YOU CAN! • ALL THE SCHOOL'S A STAGE
Scholastic Professional Books, 1998

Silent Shakespeare

Staging a scene from a play, silent-movie-style.

PURPOSE

Students act out a scene without words to explore characterization and staging.

BACKGROUND INFORMATION

When sound came to Hollywood, silent movies didn't phase out completely. They became a valuable way to explore emotions, characterization, and staging without the distraction of words. Students who are struggling with Shakespeare's language can benefit in the same way by making a "silent scene."

WHAT TO DO

Choose a scene (or part of a scene) that is more reliant on action than on words (see box on page 38). Read the scene aloud in class and discuss what's happening, who feels what emotions, and why Shakespeare included this scene in the play—what's its purpose?

Next, work together to break down the scene into a series of actions. Starting in Act 3, Scene 2 of *Much Ado About Nothing*, the actions in the scene could be described as: Don John tells Don Pedro he has proof of Hero's infidelity; Don Pedro and Claudio join him that night outside Hero's window; Margaret (dressed as Hero) appears, and so on. Write "cue cards" for these actions in the style of silent movies. These cards have a dual job of directing the actors and letting the audience know things that can't be conveyed solely with gestures.

Assign roles for the scene; the rest of the class acts collectively as a director. The actors walk through the scene without words, one event at a time. At each stop (or cue card), ask the actors what they're doing and what they'll be doing next. Ask the class to suggest movements or gestures that can help convey meaning. They can also help block out who goes where on the stage. A few small props—whatever's handy—can make acting a little easier.

Run through the scene at least twice before the actors give a final performance. How did the actors convey the meaning of the scene? Were their gestures natural or exaggerated? How do people communicate without words? (Body language, hand signals, sign language, mime, and so on.)

A variation of this activity is to freeze the action at certain points and have the rest of the class read the lines aloud.

MORE TO DO

Shakespeare Charades: Write a series of easily defined moments on scraps of paper: Ganymede pretends to be Rosalind in order to cure Orlando of his love sickness (*As You Like It* 3.2). Divide the class in half. One team elects two actors (a third actor can join them if necessary). Then they draw a slip of paper and have one minute to discuss it privately.

The actors act out the scenario, charades-style, so that their teammates can guess (1) the characters involved and (2) what the characters are doing. Remind actors that they don't have to stick to Shakespeare's script; they can improvise

TEACHING SHAKESPEARE—YES YOU CAN! • ALL THE SCHOOL'S A STAGE
Scholastic Professional Books, 1998

to get across certain words or ideas. The team earns one point if it guesses correctly in 60 to 90 seconds and two points if it does so in less than 60 seconds.

The other team then takes a turn. Teams alternate turns until all the papers have been presented. Make sure fresh actors take the stage in each round. The first two rounds may be challenging, but teams will come to develop their own non-verbal methods of communicating—waving a handkerchief as short-hand for the character Othello, for example.

Silent Scene Suggestions

Much Ado About Nothing: Claudio and friends discover "Hero" on the balcony with another man (3.2). Dogberry's guards apprehend the suspects (3.3).

A Midsummer Night's Dream: Titania wakes up and falls in love with Bottom (3.1). The four mortals fight amongst themselves in the forest (3.2).

The Tempest: The shipwreck (1.1). Stephano encounters a four-legged, two-voiced beast (2.2).

Hamlet: Hamlet follows the ghost (1.4). The players act out the murder (3.2). Ophelia's funeral and Hamlet's scuffle with Laertes (5.1). The fatal duel (5.2).

Macbeth: The witches concoct their brew (1.1). Lady Macbeth sleepwalks (5.1).

King Lear: Kent provokes Oswald (2.2). Poor Tom leads Gloucester to the edge of a "cliff" (4.1). Edmund and Edgar duel (5.4).

Romeo and Juliet: They meet at the ball (1.4). The balcony scene (2.2). They commit suicide in the vault (5.3).

Richard III: As Anne mourns her dead husband and father-in-law, their murderer, Richard, woos her to be his wife (1.2).

What If . . .

Act out "what if" situations that would change the course of the play.

PURPOSE

Students probe the moral dilemmas that face the characters by examining turning points in the plays and considering what could have happened differently.

BACKGROUND INFORMATION

Moral dilemmas are the cornerstones of drama. Shakespeare often begins a play by placing characters in seemingly inextricable situations. The characters spend the next four acts fighting, loving, and conniving their way out. For audiences, how the characters untangle these tightly woven webs *is* the entertainment.

For women characters such as Juliet, Hermia (*A Midsummer Night's Dream*), and Viola (*Twelfth Night*), the dilemma usually involves being betrothed to or pursued by someone they don't love (or hate) and being deeply in love with someone else who's off-limits. In Elizabethan times, girls generally married their father's choice, often a much older businessman who could provide stability and security. In Shakespeare's plays, the penalty for disobeying the father, as outlined to Hermia, is death, spinsterhood at a convent, or exile.

Juliet chooses pseudo-death but then dies for real. Hermia chooses exile but is later welcomed back. Viola (disguised as a boy) decides not to disobey her pursuer but not to encourage her either. Viola tries to discourage Olivia's advances as she pines for Orsino.

How would other characters (or people) handle these same situations? What might be the consequences? What unforeseen events could change the situation for better or for worse?

WHAT TO DO

Present students with a moral dilemma—a turning point—in your play. It can be something as simple as Juliet learning that her father has moved her dreaded wedding to tomorrow or Hamlet contemplating murdering the praying Claudius. Challenge students to brainstorm as many different outcomes as they can imagine.

The box below gives examples of several "what if" scenarios for different plays. To

---

"What If" Scenarios

Romeo and Juliet: What if Juliet's potion didn't work and she woke up on her wedding day? What if either Romeo or Juliet had survived? What if the Friar had announced the wedding right after the ceremony instead of keeping it secret? What if students were in Juliet's or Romeo's shoes?

Hamlet: What if Rosencrantz and Guildenstern had succeeded in assassinating Hamlet? What if Ophelia had not gone mad? What if the play took place today?

King Lear: *Ran* and *A Thousand Acres* are two movies based on *King Lear* but set in very different locales (Japan and middle America, respectively.) Where else might a *King Lear* situation take place? What if Cordelia's army had defeated England? What if Lear had a fourth daughter?

A Midsummer Night's Dream: What if Puck's love potion were permanent? What if the four lovers lived out their lives in the fairy woods? What mischief would Puck bring in a sequel to the play? What mischief could he bring to your life?

Much Ado About Nothing: What if the play took place in your school? (Who would play whom?) What if the play were a soap opera on television?

Macbeth: What if Banquo had survived? Would he have stood by Macbeth? For how long? For what reasons? At the end of the play, what if the witches tell Siward he will be king of Scotland? What will happen in the sequel to Macbeth? What if Macbeth were a modern-day senator?

spark ideas, ask students to envision various other characters (or people, including themselves!) in the same situation. Pose "what if" questions: What if Julius Caesar were a bigger believer in superstition and omen? What if you were in his shoes? What if Juliet were a modern teenager? What if, like Viola, girls in the class dressed as boys?

Have pairs of students choose one of their ideas and act out or write an alternative version of a scene.

Ask students why they think Shakespeare chose certain characters and events. Were his choices intentional or arbitrary? How does changing details affect the enjoyment or entertainment value of the play? How can it change the message or theme of the play?

More to Do

Branching Out: Stories with multiple endings, or branching stories, are good alternative projects for students who prefer creative writing to the stage. In a branching story, the reader makes choices that affect the story's plot. For example, should the character pick up the broom or walk through the door? The plot progresses according to the choices that the reader makes. If the reader chooses to have the character walk through the door, a tiger may appear. But if the reader has the character pick up the broom, he or she flies to another locale. Usually, the stories have several endings.

Turning a whole Shakespeare play into a branching story may be a little daunting, but students could focus on a scene, especially one with lots of action. The first step is to outline events as they occur in the script. Then students identify places where characters make a choice—deciding to duel, chasing after the ghost, playing a trick, wooing another character, and so on. The student writes "branches" or alternative plots for these choices, all the way to various possible endings.

My Point of View Exactly: Ask students to describe the same event from three different characters' points of view. For example, the confrontation in act 3, scene 4 of *Hamlet* involves three people: Hamlet, Gertrude, and Polonius. Have three volunteers walk through the scene (without dialogue) as you direct and describe the action.

Ask students, including the volunteers, to describe the events from each character's point of view. What did the character see? Hear? Feel? What might the character have been thinking, but not saying? Why did the character take certain actions? Tom Stoppard wrote an entire play—*Rosencrantz and Guildenstern Are Dead*—from the sole point of view of two minor characters in *Hamlet*.

A few other suggested "Point of View" scenes include: Puck watching the mechanicals rehearse in *A Midsummer Night's Dream*; either eavesdropping on a scene in *Much Ado About Nothing*; and Ariel saving Gonzalo's life in *The Tempest*.

Shakespeare, Oprah-Style

A class discussion in the form of a talk show.

PURPOSE

Using the format of a talk show, students explore a character's psychology and motivations in depth.

BACKGROUND INFORMATION

Many of Shakespeare's characters—especially the tragic ones—could easily appear on a talk show like *Oprah* and not look at all out of place.

Consider Hamlet: His father was murdered (that's one show right there), he saw a ghost (show number two), his new stepfather is his uncle (three), his girlfriend loves him but then shuns him (four), he kills a man in cold blood (five). Of course, we could also add a sixth posthumous show titled "Entire Families Tragically Killed in a Matter of Minutes!"

WHAT TO DO

The talk-show format is a lively substitute for a straightforward discussion about characters and themes. It engages the entire class, allows for creativity, and helps students connect a 400-year-old play with what's happening today.

Split the class into groups of four or five students. Each group will get a chance to "star" on the show and also to ask questions of other groups as audience members. You, of course, are the host.

Assign each group a theme disguised as a talk-show topic (see the next page for ideas). The panel for each topic should include two to four characters from the play and a suggested expert or other guest.

Group members should discuss their topics and assign roles. Then, individuals should research their roles independently, locating quotations from the text to illustrate their dilemma.

On the day of the talk show, each group has 12 to 15 minutes of "air time." Begin by introducing the guests and asking each one to make a general statement in regard to the topic. To solicit a lively debate, ask questions such as: How did it make you feel when so-and-so . . . ? How do you think your actions affected other people on the panel? What do you think you could have done differently in that situation?

Also open up the discussion to questions from the audience. Make sure the discussion stays focused on the topic and that the group onstage remains in character.

Ideas for Talk-Show Topics

ROMEO AND JULIET

Feuds: Why Do They Start? Who Do They Hurt? How Can We Stop Them? (panel: Mercutio, Tybalt, Prince Escalus, Capulet, Montague, ex-gang member)

Does Love at First Sight Exist? (panel: Juliet, Romeo, Paris, biochemist, astrologer)

JULIUS CAESAR

Kill the Tyrants: Is Assassination Ever Just? (panel: Brutus, Cassius, Antony, Calphurnia, John Wilkes Booth, or other assassin)

Do You Believe in Omens? (panel: soothsayer, Calphurnia, Caesar, scientist)

The Mob Mentality: What Happens to Ordinary People in Extraordinary Circumstances? Who's to Blame for Their Actions? (Portia, Cinna the Poet's wife, Calphurnia, General Ulysses S. Grant)

KING LEAR

Daughters Who Abuse Their Parents: How Far Does Family Responsibility Go? (panel: Regan or Goneril, Cordelia, Lear, Kent, nursing-home caretaker)

Parents Who Abuse Their Children: Can a Father Disown His Daughter? (panel: Cordelia, Lear, Fool, truant officer or juvenile probation officer)

OTHELLO

Violence and the Green-Eyed Monster: Why Do People Get Jealous? Why Do Some Jealous People Become Violent? (panel: Othello, Desdemona, Emilia, marriage counselor or psychologist)

Are People Born Either Evil or Good? or Do Good and Evil People Get What They Deserve? (panel: Iago, Cassio, Bianca, Desdemona, Mother Teresa or a humanitarian, Richard III, or other evil fiend)

A MIDSUMMER NIGHT'S DREAM

Do You Believe in Fairies (and Ghosts, and Aliens, and . . .)? (panel: Bottom, Puck, Hermia, Agent Skully from *The X-Files*, Carl Sagan)

Fate: Is Your Future Set in Stone? (panel: Hermia, Puck, Egeus, astrologer)

Do Looks Matter? (panel: Hermia, Helena, Lysander, Demetrius, Titania, Bottom)

MUCH ADO ABOUT NOTHING

Are Practical Jokes Funny or Cruel? (panel: Beatrice, Benedick, Hero, Claudio, comedian)

Double Standard: Should a Woman's Honor Matter More Than a Man's? (panel: Hero, Claudio, Don Pedro, Margaret, Madonna, Amish leader)

TWELFTH NIGHT

A Man's World: How Would a Woman Disguised as a Man Be Treated Differently Yesterday and Today? (panel: Viola, Olivia, Orsino, Feste, Gloria Steinem, Queen Elizabeth I, pirate Anne Bonny, or another successful woman in a man's world)

Women Who Love Women Disguised as Men and Other Unrequited Love Stories: How Do Victims of One-Way Love Affairs Cope? (panel: Viola, Olivia, Orsino, Malvolio, Maria, Oprah Winfrey)

THE TEMPEST

Crime and Punishment: Forgive and Forget or an Eye for an Eye? (panel: Prospero, Antonio, Alonso, Caliban, police chief)

When Is It Okay to Use Magic? (panel: Prospero, Caliban, Antonio, magician, writer)

TEACHING SHAKESPEARE—YES YOU CAN! • ALL THE SCHOOL'S A STAGE
Scholastic Professional Books, 1998

Character Cards

Following the dotted lines, cut out each character card. Then fold the cards in half and glue together.

Name:_____

Age (or approximate age): _____

Relatives:

_____

Social class:

_____

Feats and foibles:

_____

_____

Name:_____

Age (or approximate age): _____

Relatives:

_____

Social class:

_____

Feats and foibles:

_____

_____

Name:_____

Age (or approximate age): _____

Relatives:

_____

Social class:

_____

Feats and foibles:

_____

_____

TEACHING SHAKESPEARE—YES YOU CAN! • ALL THE SCHOOL'S A STAGE
Scholastic Professional Books, 1998

More Activity Ideas: Practice Makes Performance

Dramatic exercises and activities help students feel comfortable onstage.

En Guarde

Duels, fencing matches, and battle scenes play the same role in Shakespeare's day as they do in ours—quenching the human thirst for action and excitement. In a classroom, you can use the thrills of stage fighting to glue everyone's attention to the text.

Invite experts to dazzle your class with a demonstration and, ideally, a hands-on workshop using safe instruments. Contact groups that are active in your area:

❧ The directors of regional or university theaters.

❧ Local martial arts and theater combat clubs. For example, The Ring of Steel (408 Thompson, Suite 4, Ann Arbor, MI 48104-2321; rosteel@umich.edu) has prepared an eight-minute *Hamlet* scene targeted to English and drama classes.

❧ Fencers (amateur or professional). Local YMCAs and colleges often employ fencing instructors.

❧ Theater troupes that stage plays at schools. One such group is the Shenandoah Shakespeare Express (P.O. Box 1485, Harrisonburg, VA 22801; sshakespea@aol.com).

To teach students basic stage fighting on your own, an excellent lesson plan is included in the book *Shakespeare Set Free: Teaching Twelfth Night and Othello* (see resources, page 77). The theater section of your local library may have additional technical manuals for actors.

Fie Fo and Fum,
I Smell the Blood of a British Man*

Stage fighting isn't quite the same without stage (fake) blood. You can buy it by the ounce ($1.50 to $3.50 per ounce) at Halloween and costume stores, practical joke stores, theater supply companies, and shops that specialize in horror and fantasy. Also search the internet for "stage blood" or "special effects." Two of many sites are www.btprod.com or www.nightmarefactory.com.

Prefer to make your own? Creating the safest, most realistic stage blood could be a fun chemistry contest for the class. This recipe is harmful only if swallowed. Leaving out the detergent will be safer, but it may stain clothing. (Test it on sewing scraps or rags, and caution students to be careful of clothing while working.)

1 cup light Karo syrup

50 drops (about 1 tsp.) red food coloring

1 drop green food coloring (some recipes call for blue)

1 tbsp. *clear* liquid laundry detergent or dishwashing liquid

Mix all of the ingredients, increasing the amount of food coloring if needed.

King Lear 3.4.171

Sounds Good

Picture the witches scene at the beginning of *Macbeth*. The fire is crackling. The boiling liquid is "bub-bub-bubbling." The stirring stick scrapes the pot. Night animals chirp, croak, and sing. How many of these sounds could a sound effects expert make? What backstage materials might produce these sounds?

Movie, television, and radio professionals who create sound effects are called foley artists. Their job is part physics and part creativity.

Groups of students can explore the physics of sound by creating sound effects for a scene or partial scene. Like foley artists, they can experiment with a range of tools: cookie sheet (thunder); metal utensils (swordplay); cellophane (crinkle for fire or cooking sound); tissue paper (rustle of skirts or curtains); shoes (footsteps and hoofbeats), and so on. For more ideas, check back issues of *Stage Directions* magazine; 800/362-6765. But remind students that in Shakespeare's time all sound effects were live—no tapes or CDs and no amplification.

How many sounds can students make with one item? How can they control the volume? How do different types of materials change the quality of the sound?

Mob Scene

Elizabethan stages were large enough to accommodate battle scenes, crowds, multiple areas of focus (two groups talking on either side), and angry mobs. Like extras in an epic action movie, your class can practice being a stage mob or crowd—directed, but looking naturally disordered.

Why subject yourself to controlled chaos? One purpose is to make shy students less uptight about acting. In a crowd, these students can shine with just one line, knowing that not all eyes are on them.

A second purpose is to explore "mob mentality," a theme that Shakespeare visited frequently. Why do mobs act differently than individuals? (Consider Cinna the Poet—killed for having the same name as a conspirator—in *Julius Caesar*.) What feelings do mob members experience? How do mobs choose a leader?

Finally, a mob scene is a great way for students to be creative. They can add their own actions, gestures, expressions, and words to suit the occasion. Keep a tight lid on overacting and overly loud or inappropriate behavior. Don't worry about blocking out the scene for stage presentation. The goal is to enhance student's understanding of the play rather than put on a show.

To begin, students pretend that the major players are acting directly in front of them. The mob members are just reacting to events. For example, at Hero's wedding in *Much Ado About Nothing*, chaos breaks out as Hero is accused of infidelity. Announce what's happening in the scene, but don't act out or read lines. How would Hero's guests react? How might mourners express sorrow at Juliet's funeral? What happens when the Plebeians change their collective minds at Caesar's funeral?

TEACHING SHAKESPEARE—YES YOU CAN! • ALL THE SCHOOL'S A STAGE
Scholastic Professional Books, 1998

The Plot Thickens

**Wherein, post-reading or post-performance,
students further explore the themes, plotlines, and characters.**

Speak Up

Identifying crucial quotes and famous lines.

PURPOSE

A quotation game helps evaluate students' understanding of who did what, where, and when.

BACKGROUND INFORMATION

A true test of how well students understand a play is to have them identify short quotations: Who said it? Who heard it? What was happening at the time?

A deeper question is, What does this quotation reveal about the speaker? And deeper still: Why did this character choose these particular words or images?

Quotation identification questions are a common part of high school and college tests on Shakespeare. For younger students, however, the relaxed format of a game is more appropriate.

WHAT TO DO

The Speak Up game on pages 55–56 uses quotations from *Hamlet*—easily Shakespeare's most quotable play. If you're teaching another play, choose ten or more short quotations from as many different characters as possible. The selections don't necessarily have to be famous lines. Just choose lines that are very specific to or characteristic of the speaker or that pertain to the plotline.

To play Speak Up, students form groups of three, take a set of cards, and choose a level of play: (1) name the speaker, (2) name the person being addressed, or (3) answer a question.

Students take turns drawing a card from the deck and reading the quotation. The player to the reader's left has one guess to win the card. If this player is incorrect, the other player can take a guess. If neither answer is correct, the reader discloses the answer and puts the card out of play. In each round, players rotate being the reader, the first guesser, and the second guesser. When the deck is exhausted, the player with the most cards wins.

After students have finished a game, discuss the quotations on the cards. For each one, ask students to describe what's happening, who's present, where the action is taking place, and what happens before and immediately after it.

MORE TO DO

Speak Up Encore: Have students make their own game cards to extend play. An alternative version is to write up short bits of dialogue that students memorize. The reader plays one character—the first to speak on the card—and the listeners play other characters, reciting the lines from memory.

*P*lotlines

A game to help students remember the sequence of events in a play.

PURPOSE

This game challenges students to use their knowledge of the play and logic to put in order a jumbled set of plotlines.

BACKGROUND INFORMATION

For almost all of his plays, Shakespeare borrowed his plots (and sometimes whole passages) from other sources. He changed the stories to suit his purposes and then spun these old tales into literary gold. No contemporary of Shakespeare considered this borrowing plagiarism. The concept of ownership of creative art had not yet been born.

Today, many writers and filmmakers borrow Shakespeare's borrowed plotlines, changing a few details such as setting and time period to create original works—for example, *West Side Story* is inspired by *Romeo and Juliet.*

WHAT TO DO

Like Speak Up (page 46), Plotlines is a game that serves as both a review and an evaluation tool. To create the Plotlines game, break down the plot into a series of succinct statements (one per student). Include as much logical sequencing as you can—related events that must fall in a certain order to make sense. Write each statement on the plotline cards (page 57). (Don't fill in the Act and Scene lines on the top of the card. Let students fill in the blanks after the game has been completed.)

To play the game cooperatively, shuffle the deck and give each student (or pair of students) a card. One by one in the order they're seated, students take a turn. First, they read their card aloud. Then, based on the plotline, they figure out where their plotline belongs on a timeline of story events. The timeline is formed by the students themselves as they stand with their plotlines at the front of the room.

TEACHING SHAKESPEARE—YES YOU CAN! • THE PLOT THICKENS
Scholastic Professional Books, 1998

To begin, the first student simply reads his or her card and stands up to start the human timeline. The second student reads his or her card, but then must decide whether to stand before or after the first student based on the order of events in the play. If the student makes a mistake, he or she must sit down and wait for the next round. The more people standing in the timeline, the harder the game.

After progressing once through the class, start over with students who remain seated. Continue until everyone is standing and the timeline is complete. The goal is to complete the timeline as quickly as possible, ideally with just one or two passes through the class.

To add a "beat the clock" aspect to the game, play an Elizabethan tune during the game. The end of the song can signal "time's up" whether the timeline is finished or not.

A competitive version pits one half of the class against the other. Give each group an identical deck of cards. Each group member draws a card. When you say "Go!," teams scramble to complete a correct human timeline. When a team signals that it is done, everyone freezes and the students read their cards in order. If the order is incorrect, both teams continue to play. The first team with a correct timeline wins.

MORE TO DO

Storytelling: While students are standing in the timeline, have them recount the story of the play, one by one in order. In addition to reading the plot-lines on their cards, encourage them to embellish the story with details or even dialogue. To make a game of it, score one point for each fact the student adds.

As I Was Saying: Play a round of Plotlines using the quotation cards from Speak Up! Students must put the quotations in order after figuring out what's happening and when it happened.

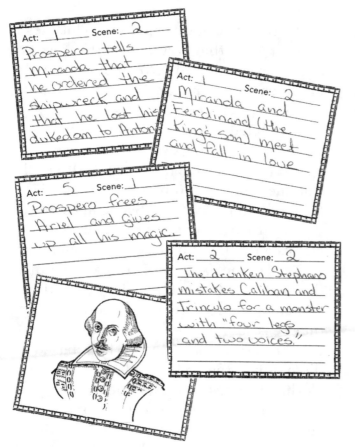

The Shakespeare Times

Create a newspaper to report on the key events and major characters in the plays.

PURPOSE

Imagine "full-team coverage" of the events in a Shakespeare play. Students expand their view of the play by reporting the events in a hard-news format.

WHAT TO DO

Students can bring alive people and events in the play by acting as reporters for *The Shakespeare Times*.

Divide the class into teams of four or five. Have each team choose an action-filled event in the play you're reading to report on (see box).

Reporters can present the news in any format—interview, feature, straight news (the five W's), commentary (editorial), or sidebar (a smaller, related story such as "Other Recent Ghost Sightings in Denmark"). These stories are "on the spot—live" and so should begin with a dateline (the time and place). Students can also create "photos" by posing as characters and taking Polaroids.

Even though the events are from a play, students should pretend that they are happening in real life. Don't forget a snappy headline or promotional hook (blurb to entice viewers to stay tuned): Sleepers Claim Abduction by Woodland Fairies; One Fake Funeral Leads to Many Real Deaths; Daughters Abuse Aging King and Father; All Hands Survive Bizarre Shipwreck.

Students can use the reproducible on page 58 as a template for their newspapers. A sample front page for *King Lear* is shown below.

Another alternative is to create a video news broadcast. It doesn't need elaborate sets; the scene could just include the principle characters, a couple of props, and a few stand-up interviews by the reporter.

MORE TO DO

Elizabethan Times: On the Web, check out an Elizabethan newspaper (www.romeoandjuliet.com/author/times)—an electronic tabloid, in fact—with brief stories about Shakespearean drama. A few sample headlines: Shakespeare a Rip-Off Artist? Juliet Disses Romeo! Nosebleed Seats [at the Globe] Go for Big Bucks!

A Few Ideas for The Shakespeare Times Coverage

Hamlet's duel with Laertes or Ophelia's funeral. (*Hamlet*)

Juliet's "funeral" and the ensuing mayhem. (*Romeo and Juliet*)

The moment the four mortals wake up. (*A Midsummer Night's Dream*)

Hero and Claudio's ill-fated wedding. (*Much Ado About Nothing*)

Viola revealing her disguise as a boy or Viola and Sebastian suspecting that they might be related. (*Twelfth Night*)

The shipwreck and immediate aftermath. (*The Tempest*)

The assassination or the appearance of Caesar's ghost. (*Julius Caesar*)

The first meeting between Macbeth and the Witches or Macbeth's death and the crowning of a new king. (*Macbeth*)

Characters Stand Accused

Judge the actions of Shakespeare's characters.

PURPOSE

Put a favorite character on (mock) trial to explore motivations and mitigating factors.

BACKGROUND INFORMATION

In Elizabethan times, capital punishment, cruel and unusual treatment, and banishment to penal colonies such as Australia's Botany Bay were commonplace. So were assassinations of rulers—even brothers killing brothers and children killing parents in order to obtain power and ascend the throne. Young offenders suffered the same punishments as adults. Kings and queens had absolute rule; they set the laws and punishments of the land. Local governments, including mayors and magistrates, enforced the laws.

By today's standards, how would Elizabethan actions and decisions be received? How does a trial by jury differ from absolute rule? How would we judge the alleged crimes of Shakespeare's characters?

WHAT TO DO

Whichever play you're teaching, at least one character desperately needs to go on trial. The objective is to explore a character's motives, judge his or her actions, and come to a consensus on a just fate (see box for character suggestions).

The reproducible on page 59 includes sample roles and charges for a trial of Brutus, who gave "the unkindest cut of all" to his friend Julius Caesar. Brutus makes an interesting subject because his motive was different from that of the other con-

TEACHING SHAKESPEARE—YES YOU CAN! • THE PLOT THICKENS
Scholastic Professional Books, 1998

spirators (does motive matter?) and because he later repented and showed remorse. The trial could take place shortly after Caesar's murder but before Brutus's suicide.

To simplify the preparation and format of the trial, structure it more like a hearing (see Shakespeare on Trial, page 68). Have students play the characters who act as witnesses in the trial. Armed with a councilor (who assists in preparing the witness) and the relevant scenes of the text, they present their evidence to the class in prepared statements. The deposition (written record of the witness testimony) is the play itself. Encourage direct citations to prove allegations of innocence or guilt.

The class can ask questions, which witnesses answer as best they can. Remind witnesses that it's okay to say, "I don't know" or "I don't remember." Also remind them that if they say it too often, they'll lose credibility.

When all testimony has been presented, everyone (even witnesses) votes on a verdict or punishment. Some Elizabethan punishments include: fine, time in the stocks, whipping, imprisonment in "the Tower," exile in a far-off penal colony, execution by hanging or beheading. Modern punishments might include: fine (or restitution to the victims), prison time, rehabilitation (counseling, for example), or execution by lethal injection or electrocution (in some states).

MORE TO DO

Monarch's Law and Order: For a more involved trial, appoint yourself as the "king" or "queen" who will render the final judgment. To begin, have a volunteer "bailiff" read the charges, the names of the defendants and accusers, and the potential punishments.

Appoint three councilors to advise the defense and three for the prosecution (or accusers). Working with their councilors, witnesses prepare and rehearse testimony based on what they know from the play. Again, point out that quoting actual text will bolster their credibility. They can also extend the facts with suppositions—guesses about their character's motives and behind-the-scene actions—and "expert" testimony from scientists, fencing experts, and so on.

You might want to create models of the evidence mentioned in the play—a bloody knife, a handkerchief, a potion, a vial of poison. Councilors and experts can examine the evidence before trial.

On judgment day, the bailiff brings forth witnesses, one at a time, to answer your questions. After answering the questions, each defense witness can make a short statement before judgment.

After all the witnesses have testified, render a final and irrevocable judgment with an explanation of your reasoning. Discuss whether students agree or disagree with the verdict.

A Few Suggested Defendants

Hamlet: Gertrude on trial for possible crimes against her former husband (What did she know, and when did she know it?)

King Lear: King Lear on trial for banishing Kent and Cordelia; Edmund on trial for being an all-round evil brother (Does his only good deed, just before dying, soften his crimes?)

Romeo and Juliet: Juliet on trial for disobeying her father and marrying Romeo; Romeo on trial for street fighting, the crime for which he was banished

Macbeth: Lady Macbeth on trial for conspiring to commit murder (Is she more or less guilty than her husband?)

Othello: Othello on trial for murdering Desdemona (He's guilty, but what's his punishment?); Iago on trial for a host of crimes (How many can you prove he did?)

Much Ado About Nothing: Don John on trial for slandering Hero and deceiving his brother Don Pedro

A Midsummer Night's Dream: Puck or Oberon on trial for wreaking havoc and interfering in the lives of humans and of Titania

---

Dear Blabby

Advise Shakespeare's characters on life, love, and loss.

PURPOSE

A "Dear Abby" takeoff challenges students to solve the dilemmas of various Shakespeare characters.

BACKGROUND INFORMATION

Characters often find themselves in impossible situations partly because of "fate" or the character of others, but often because of their own character flaws. These flaws come in many colors:

* the green-eyed jealousy of Othello
* Macbeth's blood-red quest for the throne
* Romeo and Juliet's rose-colored glasses that obscure all the hatred around them
* Julius Caesar's and Richard III's ambition to rule.

Flaws such as these can lead to poor choices with sometimes fatal consequences. Here's where Dear Blabby can help. Before learning what actually happens in the play, students can consider a character's options and dole out sound advice. Then students can read about and better understand the character's actual course of action.

TEACHING SHAKESPEARE—YES YOU CAN! • THE PLOT THICKENS
Scholastic Professional Books, 1998

WHAT TO DO

The dilemmas and conflicts in Shakespeare's plays are exaggerated for dramatic effect, but they're based on real problems and emotions. Unrequited love, obsessive ambition, teenagers disobeying their parents—these familiar themes are still being played out on TV, in the movies, and in books.

The reproducible on page 60 provides a sampling of dilemmas from tragedies and comedies. Choose a few of them to discuss, and brain-storm solutions. Once students have thought through the problem, reveal what really happened to these characters in the play:

❧ Juliet marries Romeo behind her parents' back. Their scheme goes awry, and both end up committing suicide.

❧ Lady Macbeth urges her husband to kill off the competition, but the remaining nobles finally kill off Macbeth in the end.

❧ Ophelia and Hamlet never get back together. Hamlet kills Ophelia's father by accident, which drives Ophelia mad. She commits suicide.

❧ Beatrice and Benedick (of *Much Ado About Nothing*) would have never gotten together since each is too stubborn. Fortunately, their friends played a practical joke that made one think that the other was in love. It worked and the dueling duo got married.

❧ Lysander, Hermia, Helena, and Demetrius (of *A Midsummer Night's Dream*) are under the spell of a fairy potion and so aren't responsible for their actions. Hermia's only hope is to wait for the spell to wear off.

You can also present students with letters written from the prespective of one of the characters in the play you are reading or have students write the letters. Discuss how the character's personality makes the problem worse or better.

More "Dear Blabby" Scenarios

❧ In *A Midsummer Night's Dream*, Hermia faces the death penalty if she marries the handsome, young Lysander instead of her father's choice of husband (Demetrius). Students could compare her choices, actions, and motivations with those of Juliet.

❧ In *Much Ado About Nothing*, Hero's fiancé falsely and publicly accuses her of being unfaithful at their wedding. How can she convince him of her loyalty? Or should she just dump the insensitive clod?

❧ In *The Tempest*, Prospero conjures up a storm to shipwreck his brother, Antonio, who has stolen Prospero's duchy. When Prospero captures his greedy brother, what should he do with him?

❧ In *Twelfth Night,* Viola has to disguise herself as a man, which results in Olivia falling in love with her. She can't reveal her identity. She doesn't want to upset Olivia. And she definitely doesn't want to end up married to the woman. What should she do?

❧ In *Julius Caesar*, Calphurnia truly believes that the strange signs and bad dream are omens of misfortune for her husband, Julius Caesar. But Caesar insists on ignoring them. How can she convince him she's right?

Evil Deeds and Tragic Flaws

Use an "evil meter" to rank a character's actions.

PURPOSE

Explore themes involving tragic flaws, evil deeds, and heroic character by ranking and comparing vices.

BACKGROUND INFORMATION

Name almost any vice or virtue, and you can probably attach it to a Shakespeare character: Revenge, jealousy, treachery, deceit, corruption, extreme ambition, greed, stubbornness, and loss of faith are a few of the negatives—prime tragic flaws in tragedies.

Honor, love, marriage, mercy, bravery, friendship, and empathy are among the popular positives in Shakespeare's plays.

Together, these traits paint a picture of the grander themes that run through Shakespeare's plays.

WHAT TO DO

As you discuss your play, students will discover that Shakespeare left some questions unanswered. Is it right to murder a tyrant? Are there any circumstances that justify murder? Does love or security make a better marriage?

The reproducible on page 61 asks students to rank a list of actions taken from Shakespeare's plays by how evil they are. Two spaces have been left blank for you to add situations specific to the play you're reading. Explain that there are no correct answers and that it's okay to disagree.

After students have completed the worksheet, compare and discuss the rankings. Expand the list to include mitigating factors for the "crimes." For example, item A talks about "wanting to be ruler" but doesn't mention any actions taken toward this goal. Is ambition a crime?

Explore the theme of revenge by asking students when, if ever, it's okay to kill someone else. What just actions can a person take if his father is murdered? Or her husband is assassinated in cold blood?

What other circumstances would change the ranking of the items on the list? Does understanding a person's motive help in judging his or her actions? Does knowing the person's personality or character make a difference?

Compare these items to the actions in the play you're reading. Then take time to further delve into your play by discussing the actions and motives of the characters.

MORE TO DO

Good Meter: Repeat the survey using virtuous actions and a "Good Meter." Which virtues are the most important to have? Can virtues ever turn into vices? For example, a sense of honor can lead to murder (*Julius Caesar*), love leads to jealousy (*Othello*), and bravery can lead to recklessness (*Romeo and Juliet*).

Speak Up Game Cards

Cut cards apart on the dotted line.

---

1. Identify this quote:
Not so, my Lord, I am too much in the son.
Hamlet to Claudius

---

2. Answer this question:.

What's the pun in this line?

Claudius says Hamlet isn't getting enough "sun" and Hamlet puns that he is too much of a "son."

---

1. Identify this quote:
His greatness weighed, his will is not his own,
For he himself is subject to his birth.
Laertes to Ophelia

---

2. Answer this question:.

Why shouldn't Hamlet marry Ophelia, according to Laertes?

As a prince, he owes his life to the state and must choose his wife accordingly.

---

1. Identify this quote:
Murder most foul, as in the best it is,
But this most foul, strange and unnatural.
Ghost to Hamlet

---

2. Answer this question:.

What makes this murder more "unnatural" than others?

Brother killed brother; the method was poison in the ear. Accept either answer.

---

1. Identify this quote:
I do wish
That your good beauties be the happy cause
Of Hamlet's wildness. So shall I hope your virtues...
Gertrude to Ophelia

---

2. Answer this question:.

What does Gertrude hope that Ophelia's virtues will do?
Tame Hamlet's wildness or make him sane again.

---

1. *Identify this quote:*
O, my offence is rank, it smells to
   heaven,
It hath the primal eldest curse upon't
A brother's murder!
Claudius to himself

------

2. *Answer this question:.*
As Claudius prays, what almost happens to him?
Hamlet almost kills him but changes his mind.

---

1. *Identify this quote:*
One woe doth tread upon another's
   heel,
So fast they follow; your sister's
   drown'd.
Gertrude to Laertes

------

2. *Answer this question:.*
Whose death was the "woe" just before this one?
Polonius's

---

1. *Identify this quote:*
O speak to me no more,
These words like daggers enter in
mine ears.
   Gertrude to Hamlet

------

2. *Answer this question:.*
Who enters shortly after these words?
The ghost, though Gertrude can't see him.

---

1. *Identify this quote:*
The drink! The drink! I am poisoned!
Gertrude to Hamlet

------

2. *Answer this question:.*
How is Gertrude poisoned— and by whom?
She drinks poisoned wine that Claudius meant for Hamlet.

---

1. *Identify this quote:*
There's rosemary that's for
remembrance—pray, you love,
remember—and there is pansies
that's for thoughts.
   Ophelia to Laertes

------

2. *Answer this question:.*
What does Claudius talk Laertes into doing and how will he do it?
Kill Hamlet in an unfair duel with a poisoned foil.

---

1. *Identify this quote:*
Now cracks a noble heart. Good
   night, sweet prince.
Horatio to Hamlet

------

2. *Answer this question:.*
What is the famous next line?
And flights of angels sing thee to thy rest!

TEACHING SHAKESPEARE—YES YOU CAN! • THE PLOT THICKENS
Scholastic Professional Books, 1998

Plotline Cards

Following the dotted line, cut out each character card. Then fold in half and glue together.

Act: _____ Scene: _____

_____
_____
_____
_____
_____

Act: _____ Scene: _____

_____
_____
_____
_____
_____

Act: _____ Scene: _____

_____
_____
_____
_____
_____

TEACHING SHAKESPEARE—YES YOU CAN! • THE PLOT THICKENS
Scholastic Professional Books, 1998

The Shakespeare Times

SPECIAL EDITION!

TEACHING SHAKESPEARE—YES YOU CAN! • THE PLOT THICKENS
Scholastic Professional Books, 1998

Characters Stand Accused

BRUTUS

Your best friend was Julius Caesar. You considered him an honorable, brave man. Yet you took up the knife and murdered him along with seven others.

How can you prove that you are loyal to Rome and were loyal to Caesar?

How can you explain your participation in Caesar's murder?

Why are your actions more noble than those of the other conspirators?

PORTIA

You are the wife of Brutus, the accused. You will fight to defend your husband's good name—indeed, to defend his very life.

Why should the court have mercy on Brutus?

What qualities or actions show his loyalty to Rome?

When and how did Brutus show remorse (feelings of sorrow) or guilt over Caesar's death?

MARC ANTONY

You loved and honored Caesar. You see no honor or just cause in his murder. All the conspirators, save Brutus, deserve nothing less than death. Brutus had good intentions.

How would you describe the scene of the crime after the murder?

How did conspirators show that they were disloyal to Rome?

What statements or actions prove that Brutus is more noble than the others?

CASSIUS

As the head conspirator, you're glad Caesar is dead. He was getting too powerful. He was a tyrant and wanted to be king. You, Brutus, and the others did Rome a favor by killing Caesar.

What evidence can you present that Caesar was a tyrant and aspired to be king?

Who supports your point of view?

Why is Brutus no different than the rest of the conspirators?

CALPHURNIA

You are Caesar's widow. You want death for all the conspirators. Brutus is no exception.

Why was Caesar's death simple, bloody murder?

What evidence proves that Caesar did not act like a tyrant?

How did omens and soothsayers "prove" that the murder was unjust?

PLEBEIAN

At first, you honored the great Caesar. Then you celebrated his death as a tyrant. Then you honored him again. You will go along with any decision handed down.

Do you believe that death of Caesar was just? Why or why not?

In what ways was Caesar a great Roman, a great general, and a great ruler?

Was life under Caesar better or worse than it is now?

Dear Blabby...

I'm 13 and about to get married. The problem isn't my age.
I'll be 14 in a couple of weeks. The problem is, my
parents want me to marry this boring older guy, and I'm in
love with someone else. Should I tell Dad about my boyfriend?
Should I just marry my boyfriend? Or what? By the way, my
Dad really, really, hates my boyfriend's family.
—*J.C. of Verona*

My husband could be king of Scotland. Three witch-
es said so! But he's afraid to do what it takes. I say he should do everything and
anything to obtain his goal—even step on some toes.* What do you think?
—*Steamed in Scotland*

   *Or murder pesky heirs who are in the way.

I'm in this love-hate relationship with a prince of a guy. I love him. But my
father told me to stop seeing him. So I did. But now H. is acting hateful and mean
to me. What should I do?—*Mad Maiden*

A girl I know is really beautiful. I thought she liked me. She was nice to me. I
even gave her gifts. Then she began avoiding me. She gave back the gifts. How
should I handle this?—*A Sweet and Sour Prince*

I don't know why, but every time I see B., I spout witty zingers at him. He proba-
bly thinks I hate him. He even insults me back. The truth is, I really love B. And
I could never tell him after all the things I've said. What should I do?
—*Bad-Mouth Beatrice*

Against my father's wishes, I decided to marry my deepest love—L. So L. and I
ran off into this crazy woods. Then everything got turned around. For some
strange reason, L. fell in love with my best friend H. He hates me now! He called
me a tawny Tartar!
   D., who also wanted to marry me, fell in love with H. too. H. and I got into a
really big fight. Help!—*Hurt and Confused*

Evil Deeds and Tragic Flaws

The "Evil Meter" ranks deeds from 0 (not evil) to 5 (the worst kind of evil). Think about each statement below. Then write the letters of the statements on the Evil-Meter according to their degree of evil.

a. Wanting to be ruler at any cost.

b. Murdering your brother.

c. Killing a rival in a duel.

d. Picking fights with your enemies.

e. Murdering someone out of jealousy.

f. Tricking someone into doing embarrassing things.

g. Being cruel on purpose to a boyfriend or girlfriend.

h. Assassinating someone who was getting too powerful.

i. Marrying for money.

j. Eavesdropping on a private conversation.

k. Pretending to be someone you're not.

l. Mistreating a parent who's old and helpless.

m. Lying to a parent in order to get what you want.

n.

o.

TEACHING SHAKESPEARE—YES YOU CAN! • THE PLOT THICKENS
Scholastic Professional Books, 1998

More Activity Ideas: Shakespeare Everywhere

From comic books to CD-ROMs, Shakespeare's plays have appeared in every literary form. Now, students can create their own sequels and offshoots.

Classy Comic Book

Working cooperatively, the class can create a comic book of a scene, an act, or even an entire play. Several commercial comic books are available as examples and motivators (see Act V, page 77).

Assign pairs of students, matching those who like to read and write with those who like to draw. Divide the text into as many sections as you have pairs and assign each pair a section. Students don't have to illustrate the entire section. Their goal is to get across the basics of the plot with short but meaningful phrases from the text. If available, allow students to use or trace clip-art figures (check art supply stores and bookstores).

Combine all the sections into one continuous comic book.

Classy Comic Book

HAMLET

1998

A Thousand Words

Shakespeare's characters have inspired artists over four centuries to create portraits and scenes. Harry Rusche of Emory University has compiled these works of art into a handy internet database (www.cc.emory.edu/ENGLISH/classes/Shakespeare). Here's a small sampling from his list:

Walter Deverell, *The Mock Marriage of Orlando and Rosalind* (1853)

John William Waterhouse, three paintings of *Ophelia* (1894, 1889, 1910)

Ford Madox Brown, *Cordelia and Lear* (1948–49)

Henry Fuseli, *Macbeth and the Witches* (1793–94)

Charles Leslie, *Viola and Olivia* (1859)

Philip H. Calderon, *Juliet* (1888; part of a Shakespeare's Heroines series)

The paintings are full of meaningful detail and so make great discussion props both before and after reading a play. Also consider movie posters and movie stills (sometimes available at bookstores or movie nostalgia stores.)

Son of Shakespeare

Movies based on Shakespearean plots date to the earliest days of the film industry. Not all of them are as obviously Shakespearean as, say, the Kenneth Branagh line—*Henry V*, *Othello*, *Much Ado About Nothing*, and *Hamlet* (the full text). For example, *Forbidden Planet* is a science fiction movie based on *The Tempest*. *Harry and Tonto* and *Ran* (a Japanese film) owe a debt to *King Lear*. And, of course, *West Side Story* is *Romeo and Juliet* in A-mer-i-ca.

Have students invent a modern situation that parallels a Shakespeare play. Here are a few examples:

* *King Lear* as CEO of "Made in the Shades" Eyewear; his daughters as vice-presidents, the Fool as the goofy receptionist

* *A Midsummer Night's Dream* as an alien invasion tale

* *Macbeth* set during a hot presidential campaign

* *Hamlet* as a serial soap opera: Will Ophelia obey her father and keep her distance? Will young Hamlet go completely mad?

* A scary sequel to *The Tempest* in which Caliban rules the isle

Using science fiction, drama, comedy, or any other genre, students can outline a movie plot. Make sure they include a cast list, the setting, and a beginning, middle, and end. Ask them to describe any new plot twists or changes that they've made in the basic story.

Scholastic Professional Books, 1998

Meet the Elizabethans

Wherein the players make the history and theater of sixteenth-century England come alive.

People, Places, and Events

Help students get acquainted with the Elizabethan age.

PURPOSE

Use the reproducible timeline and diagram of the Globe Theater to start a discussion and launch further inquiry into the people, places, and events of the Elizabethan era.

BACKGROUND INFORMATION

In 1534 King Henry VIII denounced the Roman Catholic religion after the Pope denied his request for a divorce. Henry then installed a new Anglican (Protestant) religion for England. His two daughters by different wives, Mary and Elizabeth, inherited the turbulent consequences of this act.

Mary I, or "Bloody Mary," lived up to her colorful nickname as she struggled and failed to restore Catholicism. Half-sister Elizabeth, a Protestant, took the throne next. While religious wars reddened the soils of France and Germany, Queen Elizabeth I used brilliant diplomacy to maintain a long and relatively peaceful reign.

While religious questions dominated many other events in the Elizabethan era, European explorers were expanding the frontiers of the New World at a dizzying pace. Spain was grabbing riches only slightly faster than legal and illegal pirates from England could take them away. The Renaissance was blossoming in Europe, where artists, scientists, and thinkers such as Michelangelo, Galileo, and Descartes were forever changing our view of the world.

WHAT TO DO

Distribute the timeline (pages 70 and 71) and Globe Theatre diagram (page 72). Use the following questions and answers for discussion starters as you study the Elizabethans. The questions include suggested activities for further investigation.

1. *What are the beginning and ending dates of the Elizabethan era?*
1558 to 1603—the 44-year reign of Elizabeth I.

Research/make a bar graph: Who was Queen Elizabeth? How did she become queen and stay queen so long? How does her 44 years compare with the reign of other English monarchs? Read a biography or historical fiction novel such as *Good Queen Bess* by Diane Stanley (Four Winds Press, 1990.)

2. *Who is Bloody Mary's father?*
Henry VIII. Her mother is Catherine of Aragon. Her half-sister is Elizabeth. Her cousin (whom Elizabeth had beheaded) is Mary Queen of Scots, the subject of numerous biographies and movies and the mother of Elizabeth's successor, James I.

Research/diagram: Draw a family tree of the Tudor family from Henry VIII to Elizabeth.

3. *In what year did England and Spain fight a famous sea battle?*
1588—the year the British Navy defeated the mighty Spanish Armada.

Research: Why did Spain attack England? Who was Sir Frances Drake and why was he a "sea dog?" (Elizabeth sent her "sea dogs"—or pirates—to raid Spanish ships and colonies. She saw Spain's sudden wealth as a threat to England. Spain attacked England in retaliation).

4. *How old was Shakespeare when he got married?*
18—young enough to need his father's permission. Shakespeare's bride was 26. He moved to London, without his family, to pursue his acting and playwriting career. He owned a share of the Globe Theatre, which eventually made him wealthy enough to build a large retirement house in Stratford.

Compare and contrast: How was life in the town of Stratford different from life in London? Write an imagined "day in the life" of Shakespeare as a teenager in Stratford and as a theater-owner in London.

5. *How many children did Shakespeare have? What were their names? Which one had a name similar to a character in one of Shakespeare's plays?*
Three—two daughters named Judith and Susanna and a son named Hamnet (similar to *Hamlet*).

Read/report: What do we know about Shakespeare? What *don't* we know? Read a biography such as *The Bard of Avon* by Diane Stanley (Morrow Junior Books; 1992).

6. *How old was Hamnet when he died?*
11. His twin sister Judith lived to age 77. Most Elizabethans died before they reached 40 years old.

Research/graph: How does this life expectancy compare to today's figures? The *Information Please Almanac* gives current figures for countries around the world.

7. *In 1601, why did all of London's theaters close down?*
The plague, a contagious and deadly

disease. By putting large groups of people in close quarters, theaters hastened its spread.

Research/Report: Using reference sources, chart the spread of plague from medieval times through the seventeenth century.

8. *Romeo and Juliet was first performed at the Rose Theatre. Where was Hamlet first performed?*
The Globe, which burned down in 1613. The Globe is the theater most associated with Shakespeare's plays.

Research/Report: Find out more about the excavations of The Globe and Rose theaters, which started in 1989.

9. *How is the Globe Theatre different from today's theaters?*
Food and drink on sale during the show, rowdy audience members, open-air (and so lit by sunshine only), bare stage, seats onstage. Other differences: No bathrooms, no intermissions, no seats for some attendees, and no women actors. All the female parts were played by boys. Players needed governmental permission to join a company.

Research/Report: Investigate famous Shakespearean actors—from Richard Burgbage—the first Hamlet—to contemporary stars such as Kenneth Branagh.

10. *A group called the Puritans sought religious freedom in 1620. Where did they go?*
Plymouth, Massachusetts.

Research: How did Puritans influence Elizabethan theater? (See Shakespeare on Trial, page 68.)

High-Class Costumes

Explore how clothing reflected social class in Elizabethan England.

PURPOSE

Demonstrate to students the rigid class structure of the Elizabethan age and how clothing revealed who people were.

BACKGROUND INFORMATION

In the Elizabethan age, Queen Elizabeth naturally set the fashion standard of the day (see reproducible, page 73). Nobles followed suit, spending outrageous sums on clothes made of imported silk and velvet. Continuing down the Elizabethan class hierarchy, middle-class citizens wore less elaborate versions of noble fashions and peasants mostly wore patchy, dull-colored wool.

These class distinctions were based on more than just economics. Sumptuary laws spelled out what styles, fabrics, and colors people of various classes could wear. Law also dictated that anyone over the age of 13 had to wear a hat.

Shakespeare's plays reflected the Elizabethan class structure. In many plays, the world goes into chaos when someone steps out of place. When King Lear loses his crown, a brutal storm breaks out and Lear ends up stripped of his clothing. When Macbeth tries to murder his way to a crown, bloody war and chaos result. The tempest

TEACHING SHAKESPEARE—YES YOU CAN! • MEET THE ELIZABETHANS
Scholastic Professional Books, 1998

in *The Tempest* occurs because Prospero's duchy has been stolen by his brother.

Today, no one is arrested for wearing the wrong color, but people still judge each other based on clothes. Consider the conflicts that arise when students wear $100 sneakers to school or how certain brands of clothing hold more status than others.

WHAT TO DO

Before beginning this activity, ask students the following questions. How do we judge strangers? What clues do we use to figure out who they are? (Clothing, neatness, speech pattern or dialect, mannerisms, knowledge, attitude, possessions, where they live, what type of car they drive, and so on.) Are all of these clues valid? If not, which ones are likely to give a false impression? Which ones are most important when judging a person?

Without revealing the color code, separate students by the color of their clothes into three groups.

* The "peasants" (P group) are those wearing muted or pastel colors and earth tones. Students without a dominant color belong in this group too.

* The "middle class" (M group) is comprised of students wearing black, white, turquoise, ruby-red, and other bright, strong colors besides purple.

* The "noble or royal class" (R group) wears purple, which symbolizes royalty. Anyone with even a bit of purple belongs in this group, regardless of other colors worn.

Invite the "royals" to sit in special chairs facing the head of the class. Place all "peasants" in the back of the class. Allow the "middle class" students to sit in the middle of the room. Can students guess what each group has in common? What sets the groups apart? What makes the people in the front of the class special? What might the groups represent?

Explain the clothing color scheme and distribute the reproducible on page 73. Add that Elizabethans also counted on fabric quality and fashion style to distinguish the classes. If students ask why peasants didn't just wear purple to look like royals, explain that not only couldn't they afford the dye (or the silk and velvet) but that dressing outside your class was also a crime.

As a follow-up, discuss with student dress codes and rules we have for clothing today. Do we have laws (or rules) against certain forms of dress today? What about the school dress codes? Or company dress codes—spoken or unspoken? For example, what if a banker went to work in blue jeans? How do these laws and rules differ from Elizabethan sumptuary laws?

MORE TO DO

How the Cast is Cast: A good example of the importance Elizabethans placed on class (and gender) is the character list of a Shakespearean play. All the royals, especially a king and his princes, top the roster, even if they have tiny parts. The rest of the men are listed in order of class, from earls to commoners and servants. Finally, the women—even major women characters—round out the bottom of the list as "second-class citizens." Only unnamed characters and spirits rank lower.

Uniform Decision: Debate the issue of school uniforms. Why are they a good or bad idea? What does a uniform reveal about the person wearing it? How do some people use clothing to look down on or look up to others? Does it matter what type of clothes a person wears?

Fashion History: Students can research sixteenth century costumes in theater or fashion history books, in the costume section of sewing pattern books, by watching movies set in the 16th century, and at a local theater company that produces plays in Elizabethan costume. Renaissance Entertainment has posted an interesting costume guide on the Internet (www.ren-fair.com/guide.htm).

Shakespeare on Trial

A look at the Puritan's attempts to close London's theaters in Elizabethan times.

PURPOSE

Explore the conflicts between the Puritans and the theater owners by holding a mock hearing with your class to decide whether to close London's theaters on moral grounds.

BACKGROUND INFORMATION

In 1601 the dreaded plague descended on London yet again, forcing the closing of all theaters. A religious group called the Puritans, led by Philip Stubbs, regarded the plague as punishment for allowing "evil" and "immoral" theaters to exist.

The Puritans fought hard to close the theaters even during non-plague years. Despite the pressure, theater patrons Queen Elizabeth I and King James I kept the theaters open. In 1642, however, a pro-Puritan government finally prevailed. Shakespeare's Globe Theatre was destroyed two years later. In 1660 King Charles II reopened the theaters, even allowing women actors on the public stage.

WHAT TO DO

After describing the conflict between theater owners and Puritans, ask whether these issues are relevant today. Define censorship (suppressing forms of expression on legal, moral, political, or military grounds). What are modern examples? How does censorship apply to Shakespeare's situation?

Assign the roles on the reproducible (page 74) to four students. Appoint two councilors to each student, and have each group prepare its testimony together. Councilors should help their witnesses anticipate counterpoints to the statements on the reproducible. Witnesses should come up with examples and details to support their point of view. For example, the Puritan witness could describe a rowdy outbreak after a play that resulted in injuries and arrest. The bear-baiter could describe how crowds love his show, in which dogs attack bears that are chained to a post or wall.

Meanwhile, the rest of the class—playing a panel of judges—generates fact-finding questions to ask the witnesses. Their goal will be to find the best possible solution to the problem.

Students may wish to research the debate in books about theater history, in biographies of Shakespeare, Queen Elizabeth, and Oliver Cromwell, and in other resources. (See Act V: Infinite Jest on page 77 and the resource box on page 69.)

On the day of the hearing, ask witnesses to step forward one at a time, state their point of view, and field questions from the judges. Councilors can coach witnesses on the answers.

After all four witnesses have finished, discuss the problem: Should the London theaters be closed down? Whether the answer is yes or no, discuss alternate solutions. For example, perhaps the theaters could eliminate beer sales or an umbrella organization of Puritans and theater owners could establish and enforce guidelines.

Compile proposed solutions into a ballot and present the ballot to the whole class (including witnesses) for a vote.

Resources: Puritans Versus English Theater

The Age of Shakespeare by Francois Laroque (Harry N. Abrams; 1993). Detailed background on Elizabethan political and social concerns; numerous color and black-and-white illustrations.

Bard of Avon: The Story of William Shakespeare by Diane Stanley (William Morrow; 1992). Biography for young adults includes a history of Elizabethan theater.

The Controversy Between the Puritans and the Stage by Elbert Nevius Sebring Thompson (AMS Press; out of print, but check the library).

The Elizabethan Puritan Movement by Patrick Collinson (Clarendon Press; 1990). A 527-page tome, but sections on theater history are relevant.

Fire and Ice: History and Biography (ourworld.compuserve.com). An online collection of religious writings by and about Puritans.

Inside Story: Shakespeare's Theatre by Jacqueline Morley (Peter Bedrick; 1994). A young-adult history of political and religious influences on English theater, including the Puritans.

The Purpose of Playing: Shakespeare and the Cultural Politics of the Elizabethan Theatre by Louis Montrose (University of Chicago Press; 1996). Chapter four of this scholarly work covers "The Theatre, the City, and the Crown."

People, Places, and Events in the Elizabethan Era

Queen Elizabeth I ruled England from 1558 to 1603. This is her era— the Elizabethan era. These are some of the people, places, and events in it.

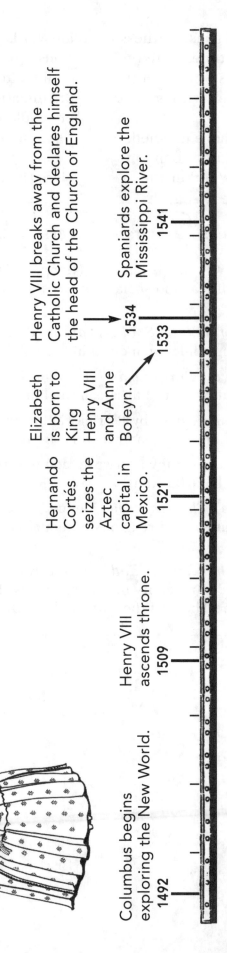

Columbus begins exploring the New World.
1492

Henry VIII ascends throne.
1509

Hernando Cortés seizes the Aztec capital in Mexico.
1521

Elizabeth is born to King Henry VIII and Anne Boleyn.
1533

Henry VIII breaks away from the Catholic Church and declares himself the head of the Church of England.
1534

Spaniards explore the Mississippi River.
1541

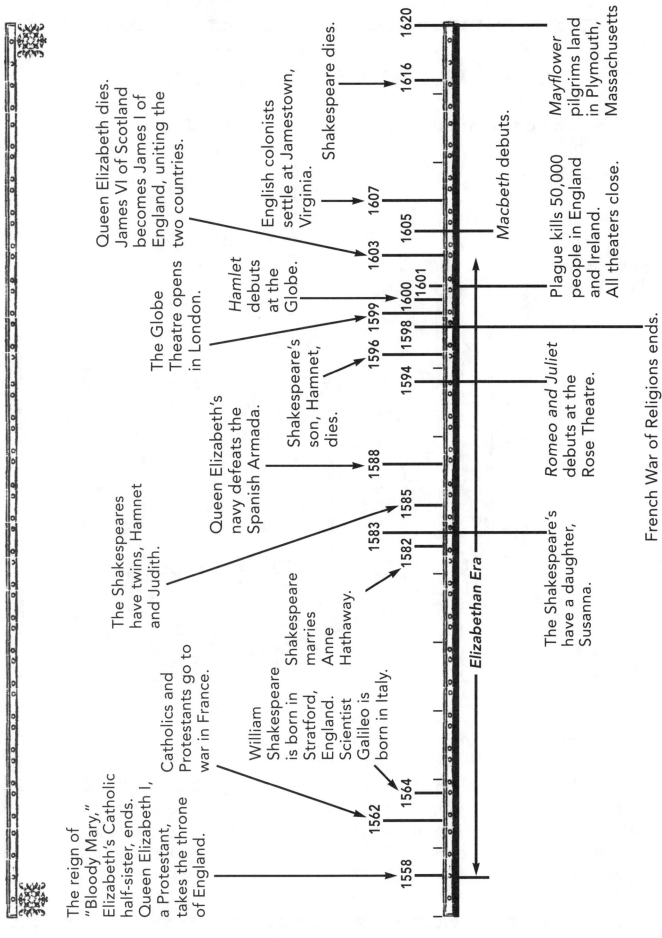

The reign of "Bloody Mary," Elizabeth's Catholic half-sister, ends. Queen Elizabeth I, a Protestant, takes the throne of England.

Catholics and Protestants go to war in France.

The Shakespeares have twins, Hamnet and Judith.

Queen Elizabeth dies. James VI of Scotland becomes James I of England, uniting the two countries.

The Globe Theatre opens in London.

Hamlet debuts at the Globe.

Queen Elizabeth's navy defeats the Spanish Armada.

Shakespeare's son, Hamnet, dies.

English colonists settle at Jamestown, Virginia.

Shakespeare dies.

William Shakespeare is born in Stratford, England.

Shakespeare marries Anne Hathaway.

Scientist Galileo is born in Italy.

1558
1562
1564
1582
1583
1585
1588
1594
1596
1598
1599
1600
1601
1603
1605
1607
1616
1620

Elizabethan Era

Macbeth debuts.

The Shakespeares have a daughter, Susanna.

Romeo and Juliet debuts at the Rose Theatre.

Plague kills 50,000 people in England and Ireland. All theaters close.

Mayflower pilgrims land in Plymouth, Massachusetts

French War of Religions ends.

Inside the Globe Theatre

What you would find at the Globe:
Open-Air Roof
Extra-Large Stage
Balcony
Groundlings
Trap Door
Elaborate Costumes
Gallery Seats

What's missing from the Globe:
Actresses
Scenery
Props
Restrooms
Intermission
Director

When a performance was scheduled flags were raised outside the theater—black for tragedy, white for comedy, and red for history.

In Shakespeare's time, women weren't allowed to act in public. Female roles were played by young boys.

The Groundlings were a tough bunch who acted like rowdy sports fans. They stood near the stage and threw apples and oranges at bad actors.

High-Class Costumes

In Elizabethan England, what you wore defined who you were. Laws dictated the strict fashions of each social class.

Queen Elizabeth wore a bum-roll (bustle), farthingale (hoop), and a tightly laced corset. Together, they made her hips appear four-feet wide and her waist appear as thin as a wasp. She also wore unrestrained jewelry, a bright red wig, a white, lead-based paste on her face, and fancy headpieces and collars.

Middle-class citizens included doctors, lawyers, merchants, and other property owners. Their colors were black, white, and bright, jewel-tones such as ruby-red. They could not wear purple, but copied other royal styles in a subdued way.

The **noble class** copied the Queen, but in more muted styles. Nobles wore imported fabrics— silk, lace, and velvet—in purple and other royal colors. Many ladies who used white paste to imitate Queen Elizabeth died from lead poisoning. Ladies generally did not corset their waists smaller than the Queen's.

Peasants wore leather, wool, and linen—all common, domestic products. Cotton, silk, or velvet were too expensive. Their colors were earth tones and pastels. They generally had one multilayer outfit, sometimes patched together from several worn-out outfits.

Shakespeare on Trial

PURITAN

 A plague is proof that theaters are evil and immoral. It is a divine punishment for sinful behavior.

The plays are bawdy and improper. No good citizen of London should be subjected to such rubbish. They corrupt people. Theatergoers become idle, lazy, or sinful.

The actors are breaking laws on the proper way to dress. Peasants wear clothes fit for royals! Unheard of! Besides, one simply should not pretend to be someone else. What's the purpose of this deceit?

Close the theaters and save our souls.

MAYOR OF LONDON

My concern is public safety. Groundlings destroy things and are loud and out of control. The theater draws criminals—pickpockets, drunks, and the like. We spend time and resources to stop them.

On the other hand, the theaters employ a lot of people. They draw visitors to London who add to the economy.

Maybe there's a middle ground. Can anyone propose ideas?

BEAR-BAITER

I run the bear-baiting ring next to the theater. And let me tell you, I'd be out of a job in two seconds without those plays— me and hundreds of other people.

Sure, some people think that what I do is cruel. But it's entertainment. The crowd eats it up.

Bad enough we got the plague closing us down. We don't need you (points to Puritan) making things worse. Live and let live, I say.

PLAYWRIGHT

I have every right to produce plays. I am writing for the Queen and her court. If you oppose theater, you oppose the Queen.

My plays don't dictate or control how people should behave. They show how people do behave. They mirror real life.

My plays entertain. The crowds like bawdy scenes and sword fights.

I have no control over the goings-on outside the theater. Cockfights, bear-baiting shows, pubs, and so on have no part in what we do.

Long live the theater!

More Activity Ideas: Elizabethan for a Day

Students can show off Elizabethan handiwork—playbills, songs, dances, and even a board game.

Ye Olde Elizabethan Playbill

Creating a playbill can be a fun final project for students after completing the play or to complement a student production. Seeing your name in print—especially in Old Gothic calligraphy print—is a shot in the arm to any aspiring actor or writer. Old Gothic and similar Elizabethan-looking fonts and clip art are available from a number of sources:

- CD-ROM collections of fonts and clip art

- How-to books on calligraphy

- Reference books of fonts and clip-art books (check art supply stores)

- Rub-on type such as Letraset™

- Rubber stamps with old-fashioned design elements.

The content of the playbill can be as simple as the name of the play, the date, and a list of players. Optional elements include a synopsis of the plot, a description of the setting, and even "advertisements" for Elizabethan products (collectible Queen Elizabeth coins, the bear-baiting ring next door to the Globe Theatre, a horse-drawn coach, a ladies' bustle, and so on).

Song Sung True

Shakespeare's plays include many songs both sad and merry that were generally set to popular tunes of the day. In some cases only the words survive; the music has been lost to antiquity. Theater companies generally compose new music following traditional styles.

Musically inclined students may want to listen to these recordings and to recordings of actual sixteenth century songs, widely available at libraries. They can also experiment with finding modern melodies to suit Shakespeare's lyrics or serve as background music for scenes such as the witches' chant in *Macbeth*. Here are a few songs to investigate:

- The fairy lullaby in *A Midsummer Night's Dream* that starts "You spotted snakes with double tongue" (act 2, scene 2)

- Either the "Sigh no more, ladies" song (act 2, scene 3) or Claudio's funeral dirge (act 5, scene 3) in *Much Ado About Nothing*

- Feste's funeral song in *Twelfth Night* (act 2, scene 4) or the Clown's song that ends the play

- The ambition song in *As You Like It* (act 2, scene 5)

- Ariel's song in *The Tempest* (act 1, scene 2)

- Mercutio's short "old hare" song in *Romeo and Juliet* (act 2, scene 3)

- The G-rated portions of Ophelia's "madness" songs, particularly "He is dead and gone," in *Hamlet* (act 4, scene 5)

- Desdemona's *Willow Song* in *Othello* (act 4, scene 3)

The Elizabethan Two-Step

Several plays include stage directions for dancing. Here's an opportunity to stage a scene with very little or no dialogue, plenty of action, and more than a handful of students involved. Choreograph your own dance or learn an authentic one (see Resources, page 77). Here are some key dance scenes:

- Romeo and Juliet meet while dancing at a masked ball; in fact, the dance steps afford them their first physical contact. The moment is tender and magical.

- In *Macbeth*, the witches dance. What might a witch dance look like?

- Beatrice and Benedick in *Much Ado About Nothing* banter and scheme at a masked ball, though Beatrice doesn't recognize Benedick in his disguise. The tone is light—all in good fun.

- The King and Helen dance in *All's Well That Ends Well*.

- The fairies in *The Tempest* and *A Midsummer Night's Dream* flit around the woods. What might a fairy dance look like?

The Ha'penny Game

A popular Elizabethan game was a tabletop precursor to Shuffleboard called Shove Ha'penny. Instead of shuffling ha'pennys (coins), use 10 poker chips (5 of one color and 5 of another), tiddlywinks, or other disks. Make a 16-by-24-inch playing surface out of corrugated cardboard or plywood. Draw 10 horizontal lines (to create 9 spaces) in the center, making the spaces just a tad wider than your disk.

To play, two people take turns sliding all of their disks (each has 5) across the playing surface. The goal is to make disks land in the spaces without touching any part of a line. When all 10 chips are on the table, score 1 point for every chip between two lines. There's no penalty for errant chips or chips on lines.

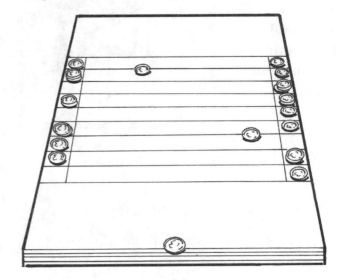

Infinite Jest

Wherein we present resources for continuing your enjoyment of Shakespeare.

Books

Ian Pollock's Illustrated King Lear: Complete and Unabridged (Workman; 1984). One example of a comic-book version of Shakespeare's plays. Most comics are abridged or rewritten; this one includes the entire original text.

The Folger Library's Shakespeare Set Free (series) edited by Peggy O'Brien (Washington Square Press). Teachers who attended the Folger's Teaching Shakespeare Institute collaborated to produce well-oiled lesson plans for various plays.

Shakespeare's Insults for . . . (series) by William Shakespeare et al. (Clarkson Potter; 1996). These lighthearted books include zingy Elizabethan epithets for teachers, lawyers, and other professionals.

Shakespeare's Insults: Educating Your Wit by William Shakespeare et al. (Crown; 1995). Zingers of a more general nature.

Shakespeare's Theatre by C. Walter Hodges (Coward-McCann; 1965). Check your library for this aging but well-illustrated history of theater for children.

Theater Games for the Classroom by Viola Spolin (Northwestern University Press; 1986). Though not directly about performing Shakespeare, these games help children relax and act naturally on a stage.

Other Media

Comedy, Tragedy, History: The Live Drama and Vital Truth of William Shakespeare (SuperStar Teachers; 1990). Two lectures on videocassette by Shakespeare scholar Peter Saccio of Dartmouth College describe Shakespeare's life at Stratford and the Elizabethan theater. Check your public library for a rental copy or contact The Teaching Company; P.O. Box 17524, Arlington, VA 22216; 800/832-2412.

The Play's the Thing, a Dramatic Introduction to Shakespeare (Aristoplay; 1994). This multilevel board game eases students into nine Shakespeare plays: *Romeo & Juliet, Hamlet, Julius Caesar, Macbeth, Othello, King Lear, Midsummer Night's Dream, Twelfth Night,* and *As You Like It.* Players begin the game as unemployed actors in Elizabethan London. Their goal is to get a part in a Shakespearean play by collecting and "performing" cards with matching characters, plotlines, and quotations. "Performances" include reading text, answering questions, or reciting text on cue. Contact Aristoplay, 450 S. Wagner Rd., Ann Arbor, MI 48103; 888/478-4263; www.aristoplay.com.

The Story of English: Volume 2 (MacNeil/Lehrer). The eight-volume video series is available for rental at public libraries; the second volume focuses on Elizabethan speech. Narrator Robert MacNeil interviews somewhat isolated English countryfolk whose accent still sounds Elizabethan and records linguists speaking in Elizabethan tongue, including passages from Shakespeare.

William Shakespeare: The Complete Works on CD-ROM (Andromeda Interactive; 1994). The main advantage to having Shakespeare on computer is being able to search through all the texts quickly and easily. Though the search function is a bit primitive and only 12 plays have annotations, the CD-ROM is a useful tool for both teacher and student. Similar collections are available on the Internet.

Internet Sites

The internet is flooded with sites directly or indirectly linked to Shakespeare. Because these sites are highly subject to change, you may want to cast your own broad net first. Search for "Shakespeare" and "Elizabethan OR Renaissance," followed by a more specific word such as "dance" or "speech." Here are a few sites of interest.

The Complete Works (the-tech.mit.edu/Shakespeare/works) includes the text of every Shakespeare play (and poetry to boot). You can search, read answers to frequently asked questions, and get a list of resources. Several sites offer similar services.

Insultor (zenith.berkeley.edu/~seidel/Shaker/shake.cgi) and two similar sites (www.nova.edu/Interlinks/cgi-bin/bard and www.tower.org) generate Shakespearean insults on demand—some taken from the text and others created at random from lists of words.

Renaissance Dance (www.UCS.mun.ca/~andrew/rendance.html and www.pbm.com/~lindahl/music_and_dance.html) sites offer historical documents on Elizabethan dance and music. For example, follow the links and you can print out the primary source text of *The English Dancing Master* by John Playford (1651)—original descriptions of dozens of English dances.

Renaissance Faire (www.resort.com/~banshee/Faire) is a fascinating training manual for workers playing the role of Elizabethan characters at Renaissance fairs. The lessons are of general interest and include Elizabethan accent and speech (with sound clips), grammar, insults, pronunciation drills, forms of address, costumes, acting tips, and historical background.

Shakespeare Classroom (www.jetlink.ne/~massii/Shakes) includes links to other sites and curriculum material prepared by Professor J. M. Massi of

Washington State University for high school and college level students.

Shakespeare Web (www.Shakespeare.com) offers links to other resources and a meandering question-and-answer database. Typical questions come from students who are writing a paper or about to take a test, and the answers come from an open community of Shakepeare lovers. The content is play specific—e.g., Why does the Fool disappear in King Lear?

Stratford Festival (800/567-1600; wsch@stratford.on.ca), the famed Ontario, Canada, theater stages plays in the spring, summer, and fall. Also available are

teacher workshops and other special programs for educators.

Theater Links (issfw.palomar.edu/Library) is a very useful list of theater-related Web sites on costume, dance, fencing, Shakespeare's complete works, and more.

Virtual Renaissance (www.twingroves.district96.k12.il.us/Renaissance) is a text-based tour through an Elizabethan village, including the marketplace, guild hall, bank, and courthouse. At each stop, visitors read advice from a citizen and learn important pointers such as which local laws to avoid breaking.

A Shakespeare Mini-Glossary

This list includes some of the more common Shakespearean words, each with an example from the text. Add your own entries as you master new vocabulary, but beware of "false friends"—words that have changed meaning in the last 400 years. For example, *bills* meant "weapons," not "paper money."

abuse: deceive "Do not abuse me." (*King Lear* 4.7.78)

advance: show "you do advance your cunning" (*A Midsummer Night's Dream* 3.3.28)

argument: topic of conversation "wilt prove a notable argument" (*Much Ado About Nothing* 1.1.236)

aspect: appearance or nature "know my aspect, and fashion your demeanour to my looks" (*Comedy of Errors* 2.2.32)

away (verb): leave "they will away presently" (*Henry IV, Part I* 2.1.60)

beggary: bankruptcy or despised poverty "Contempt and beggary hangs upon thy back." (*Romeo and Juliet* 5.1.71)

belike: perhaps "Belike for want of rain…" (*A Midsummer Night's Dream* 1.1.130)

beshrew: mild curse "Beshrew my heart!" (*A Midsummer Night's Dream* 5.1.292)

beteem: bring forth "Beteem them from the tempest of my eyes." (*A Midsummer Night's Dream* 1.1.131)

break: bring up a subject with someone "I will break with her" (*Much Ado About Nothing* 1.1.288)

close: secret "Near to her close and consecrated bower." (*A Midsummer Night's Dream* 3.2.7)

coz: cousin "I pray thee Rosalind, sweet my coz, be merry." (*As You Like It* 1.2.1)

discover: reveal "I, your glass, will modestly discover to yourself that of yourself

TEACHING SHAKESPEARE—YES YOU CAN! • INFINITE JEST
Scholastic Professional Books, 1998

which you yet know not of." (*Julius Caesar* 1.2.70)

distilled: made into perfume "happy is the rose distilled" (*A Midsummer Night's Dream* 1.1.77)

doubted: feared "Tis to be doubted, madam." (*King Lear* 5.1.6)

enfranchised: set free "I will perform it to enfranchise you" (*Richard III* 1.1.110)

estate unto: settle onto "I do estate unto Demetrius" (*A Midsummer Night's Dream* 1.1.98)

estimation: worth "whose estimation do you mightily hold up" (*Much Ado About Nothing* 2.1.22)

fair (noun): beauty "Demetrius loves your fair." (*A Midsummer Night's Dream* 1.1.182)

fond: foolish "You see how simple and how fond I am." (*A Midsummer Night's Dream* 3.2.317)

gleek: jest "I can gleek upon occasion." (*A Midsummer Night's Dream* 3.1.147)

gull: trick "I should think this a gull" (*Much Ado About Nothing* 2.3.120)

know of: ascertain or learn from "If you will know of me/What man I am, and how, and why, and where/This handkerchief was stained" (*As You Like It* 4.3.96)

likes: pleases "His countenance likes me not" (*King Lear* 2.2.93)

main: ocean "into the tumbling billows of the main" (*Richard III* 1.4.20)

meet: even "he'll be meet with you" (*Much Ado About Nothing* 1.1.44.)

misgovernment: flagrant misconduct "I am sorry for thy much misgovernment" (*Much Ado About Nothing* 4.1.96)

of your humour: in agreement "I am of your humor on that" (*Much Ado About Nothing* 1.1.122)

office: job or task "That's not an office for a friend" (*Julius Caesar* 5.5.29)

owe: possess "All the power this charm doth owe" (*A Midsummer Night's Dream* 2.2.79)

period: conclusion "the blessed period of this peace" (*Richard III* 2.1.43)

pight: determined "I found him pight to do it" (*King Lear* 2.1.67)

presently: at once "I will presently pen down my dilemmas" (*All's Well That Ends Well* 3.6.75)

several, severally: separate, separately "Our daughters' several dowries" (*King Lear* 1.1.45)

small: softly "speak as small as you will" (*A Midsummer Night's Dream* 1.2.51)

sooth: truly or truth "But in good sooth, are you he that hangs the verses on the trees" (*As You Like It* 2.3.78)

spleen: flash "in a spleen" (*A Midsummer Night's Dream* 1.1.146)

stale: decoy "for stale to catch these thieves" (*The Tempest* 4.1.186)

stay or tend: wait for "I will not stay thy questions" (*A Midsummer Night's Dream* 2.1.235)

vouchsafe: consent to "Shall I vouchsafe your worship a word or two?" (*The Merry Wives of Windsor* 2.2.40)